CW00530041

GDNF
What
Happened
Next

Also, by Andy Rollin

'GDNF What Happened To me'

Reviews:

'Truly an epic read make sure you are well supplied with tissues.'

'Well written, no flowery language just the diary of an everyday man undertaking a ground breaking trial, interspersed with subtle humour.'

'Andy has a great style in his written word with a turn of phrase which suits the situations he found himself in, perfectly.'

'Very honest and compelling true story. A must read, brilliant!'

'Read in one sitting, Its a must for anyone with Parkinsons.'

'This book was a compelling read, I could not put it down.'

GDNF

What
Happened
Next

By

Andy Rollin

Copyright © 2023 Andy Rollin

All rights reserved.

No part of this publication may be
reproduced, stored in a retrieval
system, or transmitted, in any form
or by any means without the
written permission of the publisher.

Cover image by Andy Rollin

Depicting wound of port site that
runs from ear to ear across the back
of my head, this was left after the
drug delivery system was removed.

Paperback

ISBN: 9798862134827

This book details the author's personal experiences. Opinions and views expressed are personal and may not be shared by others. All events portrayed and information given are, as far as the author is aware, accurately and honestly described, some names have been changed or assigned a random letter to protect the individual's identity. Use of this book implies your acceptance of this disclaimer.

Dedication

To all my fellow GDNFer's who risked everything in the hope of a cure.

Thank you

To Anna my wonderful wife, I may
not tell you but you make each and
every day special

Contents:

Foreword

Those of you who have read my first book will know that the GDNFer's relationship with Parkinson's UK has been difficult at times. With this in mind and so as not to destroy any of the mutual respect we now have for each other. I asked Gary Shaughnessy, Chair of Parkinson's UK Board of Trustees, if he would read this new book and gave him the opportunity to comment on it.

I believe that his reply, which follows, illustrates that despite everything including our differences of opinion we can still work together towards a common goal.

'Hi Andy

Firstly, a huge apology for taking so long to come to you. I really do apologise.

On the positive side, I've no objections to what you have written. I think you have gone out of your way to try to be balanced. Whilst I wouldn't agree with everything you have said, and others might disagree more, I feel that they are your views and you have every right to state them.

I hope the book is widely read. It kept me reading and deserves to reach a good audience

I hope all else is well

Take care

Gary'

Thank you, Gary, for your kind words, they bring with them all of our hopes for a cure.

Prologue

If you are reading this then more than likely you have a connection somehow with Parkinson's Disease. Maybe yourself or a loved one is living with the daily torment of this condition, the general public have little or no understanding of what Parkinson's really is. Sufferers are often mistaken as drunks, turned away from taxis or face the humiliation of a queue of people behind them tutting whilst they struggle to make a payment or load their shopping.

These are normal people who would just like to be able to live a normal life.

Glial Cell Line-Derived Neurotrophic Factor aka GDNF is a protein that was discovered in the early 1990's. Various companies were interested in its potential and in 1994 it was acquired by an American biotech company called Amgen Inc., following a number of studies which produced promising results.

Amgen decided to test GDNF on a group of Parkinson's patients.

Between 1996 and 1999, 50 patients had a catheter fitted in their skulls to allow GDNF to be injected into a ventricle in the brain, this study was halted early due to negative side effects and a lack of improvement in the patients. It was decided that the delivery system was at fault. In Bristol Professor Steven Gill had for many years been devising pioneering surgical techniques and devices, after hearing about GDNF he realised that his devices could be modified to improve the accuracy of the delivery of GDNF, and thereby improve its effectiveness. He set to and developed the 'Convection Enhanced Delivery System'.

In 2001, Professor Gill' began a, study into GDNF with 5 patients being fitted with the device. In 2002 he announced the successful results with all 5 patients showing improvements, the Parkinson's world was amazed, was this a cure?

Following on from this success a multi centred trial was organised including, amongst others, Bristol and Kentucky. Professor Gill enrolled additional participants and using a refined version of his delivery system started his trial. In Kentucky the trial also started using a slightly different delivery system, although both sets of patients showed improvements the   Bristol patient's improvements were greater, this was attributed to the refined delivery system used in Bristol.

Around the same time Tom Isaacs, who co-founded 'The Cure Parkinson's Trust', was carrying out a 4,500-mile walk around the UK coastline to raise money for research into a cure for Parkinson's, as he travelled, he visited hospitals and research centres along the route. When he reached Bristol, he met with Professor Gill and was impressed with the work being done with GDNF and their achievements, he realised GDNF's potential and put all his efforts into its development, working in partnership with Professor Gill championing GDNF, trying to move it onwards. The future was promising.

In 2004, GDNF suffered a devastating blow. Firstly, it was discovered that some of the patients had developed anti-bodies and also there was concern when monkeys used in another of Amgen's studies were discovered to have suffered irreversible brain damage. Amgen decided to halt the trials immediately and withdraw the GDNF infusions. The American patients were outraged that their 'cure' had been removed when it so clearly worked, these American patients fought a lengthy campaign, including a legal battle, against Amgen to have their infusions restored, but they were not successful. It was later revealed that the monkeys had received an extremely high dose of GDNF.

GDNF was now in the doldrums and it was becalmed for several years.

In January 2010, Amgen licenced the rights to GDNF to a company called

Med-genesis who were very keen to see another clinical trial. Eventually in 2012, Professor Gill and the Bristol team announced that that there was to be a new trial held in Bristol, which would be using a new delivery system, designed by Professor Gill, which involved tubes being implanted in the brain with pin point precision thanks to the assistance of robotics. These tubes ran to a small port which was placed just behind the ear, through which the GDNF was infused.

The trial was to assess if GDNF could slow, stop or reverse Parkinson's Disease. It began with a small pilot group of 6 participants to assess the safety of the surgical technique and the infusion of the GDNF.

By 2015, 41 people with Parkinson's had been recruited to be participants in the full-scale stage 2 trial, and I was one of them.

My tale begins here.....

Introduction

Hello,

I'm Andy Rollin, if you've read my previous book then thank you, please feel free to move on to the next chapter. If you haven't or would like a recap read on.

I was 47 when I was diagnosed with Parkinson's. 5 years later I had the opportunity to take part in a ground-breaking clinical trial to see if something called GDNF could slow, stop or reverse Parkinson's. At the end of the trial my Parkinson's was indeed reversed and the majority of the participants were also improved.

Despite this the trial failed to meet its primary end point, it had failed to prove that GDNF worked. This was, I believe caused by the use of the UPDRS scoring system. The Unified Parkinson's Disease Rating Scale was originally developed in the 1980's and has become the most widely used clinical rating scale for Parkinson's disease. I believe that this is an outdated assessment measuring tool, which failed to capture many of the improvements reported by the participants because they were difficult to quantify.

The participants were abandoned and GDNF was again consigned to the doldrums. The participants believed so strongly in GDNF's potential that they formed 'The GDNF Participants Group' a.k.a. 'The GDNFer's' a group of strangers, who had been forbidden to talk to each other about the trial, brought together by the fear that to do nothing was the worst thing they could do and their knowledge that GDNF most definitely worked and was disease modifying, it was just that the scientists had yet to prove it. Our objectives are, firstly to help develop more suitable assessment tools which will accurately measure improvements in Parkinson's patients, to ensure that future participants in clinical trials have a better experience than we did and to ensure that GDNF has another chance to be proven in a clinical trial, which would ultimately make this life changing treatment available to Parkinson's patients.

This is proving to be a saga of truly epic proportions and in the years to come in the hospitals and clinics of the medical world, in the darkened corridors and consulting rooms of Neurological departments, neurologists and Parkinson's nurses will speak in hushed tones as they reveal to Parkinson's patients the secret of GDNF, to tell the tales that have been passed down through the generations of the GDNFer's and of their struggle with the scientific community, to finally get GDNF recognised as the wonder drug that it truly is.

Peace in Our time

We re-join my adventures on Saturday 1st February 2020 at The Holiday Inn, Filton, Bristol. The GDNFer's have had a successful re-union the previous day and are now in a meeting with Parkinson's UK, hopefully building bridges so we can move forward together to bring GDNF onwards as a treatment for Parkinson's.

Jayne, beloved leader of the GDNFer's, calls for order and the meeting begins, representing Parkinson's UK are S, G and C. Jayne asks the question.

'How near do Parkinson's UK think we are to launching a new trial?'

This has completely thrown S, he thought we were meeting to discuss the groups grievances with Parkinson's

15

UK, obviously he has prepared for that and Jayne's question is unexpected.

Eventually he answers.

'We are waiting to receive the protocols and as soon as we receive them, they will be fast tracked. Although this process is still likely to take several months.'

This is the exact opposite of what we were told last night by Steven Gill who also updated us on the progress or lack of it for the phase 3 trial. As the trial will be run outside of the NHS a company has had to be formed to run it comprising Steven Gill, Renishaw and Med-genesis, the protocol for the trial has been written and is awaiting submission to the regulatory body. Unfortunately, Renishaw and Med-genesis are in dispute about who gets what when GDNF is proven and available as a treatment, they are currently in stalemate and all progress has stopped.

As well as the dispute the other problem is the fact that Med-genesis have a small supply of GDNF, sufficient to start the phase 3 trial but it must be used by September 2021 and it would take about a year to manufacture more supplies. In order to make use of the GDNF the trial has to start by August 2020. Given the time needed for recruitment of participants etc. it means that the protocol must be submitted within the next few weeks, usually Parkinson's UK, who are going to be funding the trial, will not look at the protocol until it has been approved which will take 3 months. Apparently, there is no reason why the submission and Parkinson's UK looking at the protocol can't happen at the same time.

Jayne had asked Steven Gill.

'What can we do to help.'

He replied.

'Get Parkinson's UK to agree to look at the protocol now, if this deadline is missed then the trial is unlikely to ever happen.'

Jayne shares this update with S, who at first denies having been asked by Steven Gill to look at it.

He then says.

'That's not a problem anyway, if we miss the deadline, it's ok, all it means is we have to wait for more GDNF to be manufactured.'

This will delay progress by at least a year, the group are outraged and they bombard him with questions.

He declares.

'I don't know why you are getting at us, we're the good guys.'

The group turns into a mob.

The simple truth is that since the trial we have been promised so much action but nothing ever happens, we have heard this story before. S takes stock of the mood in the room and changes tack; he agrees to write to all of the involved parties spelling out the need for them to see sense and agree terms before everything is lost. He will try to send it by the end of next week!! Jayne reminds him of the need for urgency.

The meeting breaks up. The original agenda, our grievances, will have to be dealt with another time. It has been a great success and the group handled the shocking news expertly under Jayne's guidance. Hopefully the stalemate can be resolved, and things can move forward.

So, Parkinson's UK are expecting the protocol and will deal with it promptly. And S is sending the letter to the other parties, to paraphrase Neville Chamberlain.

'There shall be GDNF in our time.'

I just hope that S's piece of paper is more successful than Neville's was.

The Letter

Parkinson's UK contact Jayne soon after the meeting, firstly to thank her for chairing the meeting and to say that they are pleased with the progress made both on the GDNF front and in terms of our relationship. This is an important moment as we need each other to push GDNF forwards. Personally, I feel that the meeting allowed us to clear the air and I left hoping that we can start to work constructively together.

Parkinson's UK have also included a draft of the letter that is to be sent to the interested parties.

In this letter they call on the key parties to move research into GDNF forwards to enable a further trial of GDNF for

Parkinson's to start as soon as possible. They state that there were encouraging signs that GDNF may be helping to reawaken and restore damaged brain cells and that many participants have reported life-changing and continued benefits. They believe that GDNF holds enormous hope for delivering a therapy that could slow, stop or even reverse Parkinson's but to move things forward we urgently need a new and robust clinical trial.

Calling upon the parties involved to redouble their efforts to reach agreement on a viable clinical trial proposal.

This will be sent alongside a letter from the participants group, which is a more emotional letter and tells of our passion to see GDNF move onwards, thanking the interested parties for their work and commitment so far and begs them to come together one more time to try and resolve their differences.

Parkinson's UK have asked for comments or revisions to their letter. The GDNF participants group are split between those who think the letter is fine and those who think it's weak and needs beefing up. The group make some suggestions and Parkinson's UK revise their letter to be more forceful. The letters are sent and Jayne reports back that they have been received, however the situation is extremely sensitive not just between the interested parties but also between us and Parkinson's UK as S does not like the fact that we ask questions and demand answers. He would prefer us to be submissive, he's never met patients who answer back. Things are on a knife's edge and there is some disquiet amongst the group about how sincere Parkinson's UK really are.

It is now 18th February and I receive an update email from Jayne, to summarise the contents 'NOTHING HAS HAPPENED.'

13th March, negotiations between the interested parties are still ongoing, it seems that no one is prepared to give any ground, things are not very hopeful, I think we may already have passed the point where the existing supply of GDNF could be used.

Have just discovered that at the end of March, Alan Whone is to give a talk about the involvement of Bristol Neuroscientists in the GDNF trial. Taking place at the Will's Memorial Building in Bristol, I pass the news onto Jayne and Darren and we all manage to obtain tickets. This will be an excellent opportunity to promote our cause as everyone attending must have some form of interest in GDNF.

Only a week later we learn that due to the ever-worsening Covid 19 pandemic Alan's talk has been cancelled. The whole country is now in total Lockdown, Boris has given a press conference stating that everyone should stay at home until told otherwise, only going out for essential shopping.

Looks like an enforced holiday for me, this will give me the opportunity to do something I have been thinking about for a while.

A Book & A Good Idea

The lockdown begins, this is serious stuff, people are panic buying in the shops. Anna and I went to our local Tesco today only to find a line of shopping trolley warriors snaking all around the shopping centre and back on itself, it would have taken us 2 maybe 3 hours to get into the store. So, we go home, and I return when Mr Parkinson's awakes me the next day. This time it is different, and I can count the number of customers on my hands which is just as well as there is hardly anything on the shelves. Why have people been panic buying toilet paper?

Having failed in my duty to bring home provisions for my family. I start looking through all the emails and paperwork relating to the trial, I want to make a list of events that happened while I can still remember them. After a while my list has evolved into a series of paragraphs which have become very large.

As I read the emails again all sorts of memories are popping into my head. Each one triggering another, before I realise it, I have written a couple of thousand words and it's just pouring out of me. I print the first half a dozen pages and ask Anna if she will read it, I watch as she does so, every now and again she smiles or has a small laugh.

'It's good.'

She says.

It is now 6th April 2020, and I receive an update from Jayne, she warns us that the situation remains volatile and is complex.

She continues.

'As you are probably aware Steven Gill has set up a company called Innervate, with the intention of working with Med-Genesis and Renishaw as partners to set up and run a lead in trial, which would hopefully result in a full phase 3 trial. Crucially, the three parties have been unable to reach agreement, on contractual terms we believe, despite a number of attempts. Now neither Steven Gill nor Renishaw have been able to find a way to work alongside Med-Genesis. This would appear to be an irrevocable situation.'

This is not really a shock, there was no agreement in February and the only thing that has changed is a plea from Parkinson's UK and us, it is and always has been a business decision.

We are left with a mess which Jayne attempts to put into plain English.

'The Intellectual Property Rights of the delivery system concept (Innervate), and the Patent for design and manufacture process (Renishaw) are secure and the two companies have agreed to work together.

Similarly, the Intellectual Property Rights for the current GDNF are owned by Med-Genesis; the associated licence to manufacture has now lapsed which means any pharmaceutical company could manufacture this form of GDNF.

Both Med-Genesis and Innervate/Renishaw are now at liberty to make their own proposals to Parkinson's UK for a trial.'

Apparently, Steven Gill has been looking for new partners and has found a pharmaceutical manufacturer, who could supply the current form of GDNF within 18 months.

He has also been in talks with a researcher from Helsinki, who is working on a more recent form of GDNF which is thought will last longer in the body and is also thought to be less likely to provoke an immune system response. This could mean less frequent infusions and reduced doses to achieve similar results.

Unfortunately, this new GDNF is only at the preclinical trial stage. Steven Gill has the capability and facilities to carry this out in Bristol but would require funding of about £300,000 and it would take up to two years before a phase 1 trial could be considered.

All of this is so frustrating, we were so close and now everything is slipping through our fingers. The new form of GDNF sounds promising, but it's so far away from clinical use, perhaps 10 - 15 years. If I knew his phone number, then I would ring Victor Kiam and ask him 'to buy the company.'

 A few days later I receive an email from Lesley. Jayne has asked all of the Working Party to contact a few participants to get their views on where we go from here, things have changed since we first came together and they want to know that they are still in tune with us. I reply giving my view that GDNF as we know it is dead in the water and perhaps, we should take a step sideways by supporting Steven Gill with his work with the new form of GDNF.

I close by telling her that I've been thinking about our adventures when we used to share an infusion room.

I say to her.

'Don't laugh but I've started writing a book about my GDNF experiences. It's not going to be an epic but so far I've got just over 10,000 words and I'm at about week 38 of the trial, it starts when I was diagnosed with a brief history of how I got to be on the trial and it could end with the contents of Jayne's email.'

Lesley kindly offers help with memories, but that is not a problem, no writer's block for me. At the moment only a couple of family members have had sight of it, they say it's good but I would like someone else's insight.

So, I ask Lesley if she would mind reading a couple of chapters, I value her opinion and she will know if I'm writing nonsense as we shared the experience of a clinical trial. She readily agrees and promptly receives the first few chapters by email.

I need to check a couple of facts with Jayne and email her to say how I'm spending my time; I take the opportunity to ask if she would read the sections that relate to the group to check that I've got my facts right. I want her to be brutally honest and tell her I will not be offended, whatever she says.

It is Sunday afternoon and I have just received an email from Lesley, I nervously open it, not knowing what the contents will reveal, have I been wasting my time?

She begins.

'Hi Andy, I have just spent a very pleasant afternoon reading and re-reading the section of your book that you sent me,'

This is promising I think to myself. I continue to read, she is very complimentary and offers to read more if needed, how wonderful, someone likes my work.

A couple of days later I receive Jayne's reply.

'Christ Andy, this is powerful. It had me laughing one minute and crying the next!! My honest opinion is that it is perfect.'

I'm delighted by her response as I know she would tell me if it was gibberish. The knowledge that two people that I respect and admire enjoyed the book, spurs me on to complete it.

I continue writing. After 10 days my 'list' has turned into 27,000 or so words, it's finished all I have to do is sort it into chapters and check it through. I am going to self-publish it through Amazon, in order to do so I have to re-format it, design a cover and so on.

This process is taking longer than I imagined, there are so many aspects to it; which font do I want? what size? Chapter headings and so on? The cover is revisited several times with different layouts and colours. Suddenly it's ready. So I submit it to Amazon to be electronically checked to ensure that it complies with all of the formatting requirements and thankfully there's a spell check.

It's all ready to publish so I order a few proof copies as although it's been checked several times, I want to have a physical book in my hands. A week or so later a parcel arrives, I take it into Anna and open the box excitedly, remove the reams of packaging and there it is.

My book.

I pass a copy over to Anna, who begins to skip through it commenting on the look of it and so on. As she does so a most peculiar feeling sweeps over me, a mixture of familiarity because I've virtually seen the cover so many times and now it's here in front of me. And wonderment that my words are now written down and available for anyone to see. I pick one up and turn it over and read the synopsis.

'Andy was diagnosed with Parkinson's at the age of 47, but surely that's something old people get?

There is no cure for Parkinson's.

I forward a copy to Jayne and Darren for their perusal. A few days later Jayne emails and is very complimentary about the book, but is concerned about Parkinson's UK's reaction to it and asks us over to discuss the matter the following Sunday.

We arrive mid-afternoon and as usual are warmly welcomed, it's a lovely sunny day and we sit and watch the boats go by. Jayne is concerned that Parkinson's UK may set their lawyers on to me.

Darren says

'Be brave, just go for it, as actually the full truth is much worse.'

 I also have my concerns regarding Parkinson's UK, but as Darren says.

'It's only the truth.'

I still have emails etc. to back me up. No one from Parkinson's UK is named, I have put a disclaimer in the front and if they did get funny about the book, they would be the bad guys for hounding a participant in a trial they funded. In the current climate with fund raising hit by the Covid 19 situation would they want any adverse publicity? plus would they be all that worried about a book that is only likely to sell a few copies.

The conversation moves on.

I glance around, taking in the river, the boats and the countryside beyond. I am reminded of how much we enjoyed the summer GDNF event which Jayne and Darren hosted last July. So, I tell them.

Jayne looks at me and then says.

'You know that after last year's summer event we said never again.'

I look at her and can see how excited she is, she continues.

'Lesley has had the most wonderful idea'.

She explains that Lesley had been reading Tom Issacs's book, 'Shake Well Before Use', which details his epic walk around Britain's coast, a distance of some 4,500 miles, and was struck by his wonderful sense of humour and his total commitment to the cause. His achievement was nothing short of amazing and very brave. She was left thinking that maybe, somehow, we could build on this by replicating his journey, with the group covering the distance between themselves.

Apparently, Lesley emailed Jayne with the idea a few days ago and that is all they have been talking about since.

It had been planned to name the event after Tom, but following a discussion with his widow, Lindsay, it has been decided not to use his name and that it will be a GDNF Participants Group event.

This is an absolutely wonderful idea, and in the absence of any form of way forward for GDNF at the moment 'The Challenge' will raise money, and more importantly, public awareness of GDNF. It will have to be a spectacular as it may be GDNF's final chance to prove itself to the scientific world.

They want to involve as many GDNF participants as possible, together with the main Parkinson's charities and various other people who have some form of link to the Parkinson's world. To exclude no one and include everyone, to all work together as a unified team.

I know that they have the drive and determination to make this Challenge a success.

So, when Jayne asks.

'Would you like to help out?'

I sit back and think how easy it would be to let someone else do all the work, but no, I want to be involved, we need 'to stand up, shout out and be counted.'

'I'm in.'

I say.

Hope & Publication

Ever since our last meeting with
Parkinson's UK on 1st February, which
resulted in the letter that was
ultimately ignored by the interested
parties. Jayne and the group Working
Party have been working together with
Gary, the chairman of the trustees for
Parkinson's UK. They have made
serious in-roads into insisting on a
"default place at the table" to ensure
that the GDNF participants will be
included in any future discussions that
comprise of progress with
Neurotrophic Factors, like GDNF.

Since Gary's arrival Parkinson's UK's
attitude towards the group and GDNF
has completely changed for the better
and I don't think it's a coincidence, he's
certainly a driving force and has such a

positive outlook. He has called a meeting with the overall participant group for today, 26th June, he has asked the Deputy Research Director to come and talk to us and hopefully explain about the different sorts of neurotrophic factors and how they work in the brain. Also, why Parkinson's UK feel it is still feasible to be looking at another phase 2 trial for GDNF.

The meeting has just finished and I must say that Parkinson's UK have gone up in my estimation several notches. They are making all the right noises about moving GDNF forwards. The words 'fast-tracked' were mentioned, although on past experience this will still means several years, but at least it's a move in the right direction. This is good news; I think that the new broom must be sweeping clean.

Did you know that 28th June is the day that Archduke Franz Ferdinand of Austria, heir to the Austro-Hungarian throne and his wife Sophie, Duchess of Hohenberg were assassinated in Sarajevo on 28th June 1914.
It was this act which ultimately led to the First World War. It is now also the day my book is to be published.

I wake early as usual and log on to Amazon, type GDNF into the search bar and there it is, my book!

I scroll down, it's available in paperback and as an ebook, there are pictures of the front and back covers, a link to my author's page, book description and so on. Of course, I know all of this already because I uploaded it myself, but it's still a shock to see it all there ready for someone to buy the first copy.

I have created a short video to promote the book which I post on Facebook and Jayne has kindly offered to include a mention of the book in the latest participant group update. Within hours I am getting 'likes' and 'comments' from the Facebook posting not just from family and friends but also from complete strangers, some who have heard of GDNF and are interested in information about it and others who never knew it existed but are interested. The common theme is a desire to find out what happened and if the treatment was successful. My inbox is full to overflowing with messages wishing me good luck and congratulations.

Within a few days 20 copies, a mixture of eBooks and paperbacks, have been sold. I receive emails from some of the participants telling me how much they enjoyed the book, of how reading it refreshed their own memories and how similar their experiences were. After knowing these people for around 5 years and meeting on a regular basis this is the first time that we have heard each other's stories.

It's almost as if we are all still on the trial and not allowed to speak to each other about it, if so many of us had such similar trial experiences, then how could the results have been deemed to be negative. For the assessment tools used to have missed all of these improvements, not in the ability to perform a test but in the quality of everyday life. To be able to put your own socks on, button a shirt, to do the simplest of things with ease, these are the things that make life better, more normal. If you can stamp your feet, touch your nose or make a fist then that's great, but not important. The provision of a more suitable assessment tool is vital. Before another trial is set up to fail.

My book's popularity continues, copies have been sold both in America and Canada, I go to my GP's for my annual check-up only to be greeted by the nurse telling me that she has ordered a copy. I go to see a regular customer at work and she asks me to sign her copy. An elderly couple who have read it contact Lesley to make a large donation to Darren's fund because they were moved by it. I am truly overwhelmed by people's reaction to my story.

The Working Party

23rd August 2020, I have received an update email from Jayne today. She has used the opportunity to give the group details of the proposed Challenge.

In 2002 – 2003 the late, great Tom Isaacs completed a walk around Britain's coastline, a distance of 4,500 miles. It was during this walk that Tom met Steven Gill and his passion for GDNF began.

In a nod to Tom, the Challenge will take the 4,500 miles and divide it by the 42 trial participants, there will be 42 teams each led by a participant or their representative who will cover the distance of 100 - 120 miles, using any method as long as it's under their own power. The event will take place between the 1st - 10th April 2021 and will end with a big celebration to mark, hopefully, the successful outcome.

Jayne would like to include all of the main Parkinson's charities, scientists, pharmaceutical companies together with people living with Parkinson's internationally. To bring the Parkinson's community together to unite against this terrible disease.

A launch date of 1st October would give six months to pull this together and to start raising funds which would be used specifically for research into Neurotrophic factors, such as GDNF, with each team choosing which Parkinson's charity would benefit from their endeavours.

She is setting up a 'Working Party' to organise the Challenge and remembering that I expressed an interest, is inviting me to join the group. In the past I would not have wanted to be involved and would not have joined. However, I'm so passionate about GDNF that I will do almost anything to try and push it onwards. So, I agree.

A date is set for Wednesday 9th September at 6.00 p.m., it is going to be a 'Zoom?' meeting over the internet. Lesley forwards an agenda to me.

AGENDA

1.Bringing the challenge to life

2.Administration (Meeting frequency, Roles)

3.Ideas for launch (Mind map)

4.Engaging the participants in the challenge with a reunion (Potential date, venue, logistics)

5.Cure Parkinson's and Parkinson's UK suggestions for their representatives to join

6.Any other business

This is certainly going to be a new experience for me, what's a 'mind map?' 'Roles' what will this entail? I feel completely out of my depth. What am I doing?

It's Wednesday, just before 6.00 p.m. and I'm waiting to be let into the meeting. It has taken over an hour to get this far and I'm not convinced that this Zoom thing is going to work. The screen changes and I can see Jayne, she's talking to me.

'Andy, we can't see or hear you, you have to activate your camera and microphone.'

I think that Jayne must have Harry Potter's marauder's map, she can't see or hear me but she knows I'm there. Desperately I search the screen for some clue as to what she means, eventually I move the mouse over the correct part of the screen. And 'as if by magic,' like Mr Benn's shopkeeper, a task bar appears out of the blur on the screen. I can now see a camera and a microphone symbol both with a large red cross over them, which I click on. My invisibility cloak slips and the black box on the screen, which previously only had my name on, comes to life, and I'm there. I've joined the meeting. I look at the screen which has divided into several small rectangles, each rectangle allows a snapshot into its owner's life. This is live video; I take a quick look around; everyone is well attired and their makeshift studios pleasant. I make a mental note, must get dressed before meetings and no pyjamas!

There are a few minutes of chit chat followed by the usual introductions, attending are Jayne and fellow participants Lesley, Bob, Vicki, Nic and Jane, also Janet who is Gary from Parkinson's UK's wife.

Jayne begins by thanking us for attending and then refreshes our minds by running through the basic idea for the challenge.

Jayne pauses briefly before going around the virtual room asking us all what talents we possess that may be useful to the Challenge. As she gets nearer to me, I am racking my brain to think of some deeply hidden talent that I possess. When it's my turn I say.

'I have no talents, only my enthusiasm, if you give me a task, I shall carry it out to the best of my ability.'

Jayne replies by saying.

'I like that.'

The subject of roles is raised and after some debate the following were agreed and accepted: -

Jayne - Group Leader.

Janet - Overseeing the project as a whole and ensuring cohesion and timely action.

Nic – Counsel, ensuring the challenge stays within the strategy.

Vicki - Co-ordinating social media.

Lesley – Secretary.

Bob -   Maintaining liaison with the wider group and organisation of group reunion.

Andy (me) - Recruitment of Participants, Liaison with participants to encourage participation.

Jayne's sister Gina has expressed an interest in joining us so it is agreed to ask if she would take on the role of treasurer.

Jayne suggests that Gary, who is Chair of the Board of Trustees, for Parkinson's UK, should be invited to join the Challenge Working Party. One of the first times he met the representatives of the group was at a meeting at Jayne and Darren's house, also there were Lesley and Colin. They were all very impressed with him.   He came across as totally honest, reliable and down to earth, certainly a man who did not suffer fools gladly, but would stand by those he believed in. He has been like a breath of fresh air and has really made it his mission to make Parkinson's UK listen to us. He was appalled at the treatment we had received and was determined to make sure it didn't happen again. That meeting with him lasted several hours, and he made it clear that he would not stand back and allow Parkinson's UK to continue treating us badly and he has been as good as his word.

He really will be an asset to the Challenge.

I raise the idea of a Challenge pack which would include GDNF based items such as a t-shirt, cd of Shine(the GDNFer's attempt at a Christmas number one), dvd of the trial documentary, copy of my book. Unfortunately, in order to provide this, we would have to charge an entry fee and concerns are expressed regarding if we can ask the participants to pay to join the Challenge when they have already given so much.

The meeting is drawing to a close and as part of my new role I am tasked with emailing the trial participants to ask if they will commit to the Challenge. A few days later and after several drafts I send out my first Working Party email.

'Hello,

I have been asked to approach all of the participants from the stage 2 GDNF trial to invite all of you to join together once more to push GDNF nearer to the winning post by participating in the GDNFer's latest event 'The GDNF Participant Unifying Challenge. 'The purpose of this event is not only to raise money and the profile of GDNF, but also to celebrate what all of the participants have helped to achieve for future clinical trial participants, the respect now shown to us from within the scientific community and all the personal triumphs we experienced thanks to the wonder of GDNF.

The challenge would be for the remaining stage 2 participants to travel a distance of 120 miles by walking, running or cycling etc. over a 10-day period. Don't worry if you think it would be difficult to complete on your own you can have a team to help you or a 'buddy' who would represent you and participate in your name. You can join in simply by consenting to your name being used by a buddy. The important thing is that we are all working together again.

The challenge will take place between 1st – 10th April 2021 with an event on the 11th April to celebrate our success. At the moment plans are still being finalised, but we would like you to become involved at an early stage and would welcome any input, there are still spaces on the challenge Working Party if you want to be closer to the action.

Please think about being involved and then using the attached form let us know if you would like to be part of something very special.

Best Wishes

Andy Rollin'

Within a few days I receive positive responses from several trial participants all keen to be a part of the 'Challenge.' We had better get this right.

Chafing, Meetings & Assessments

Anna and I are both a little concerned about our fitness levels. Doing a physical job, I can fool myself that I am reasonably fit, the truth is somewhat different and I have no idea if I can actually carry out my part of the challenge.

It is decided that we should start training. So, one bright sunny day we go to 'Newark Park', a local National Trust property which has been closed due to Covid 19. But has recently opened up its grounds, tickets are limited and you have to book but we managed to get some. So, off we go.

There are several footpaths to choose from, so we follow the trail down the valley to a river side meadow, where we stop and eat our sandwiches. Later returning to the car park via another trail. We've been gone around 3 hours, covered about 4 miles and had a thoroughly good time.

Over the next few weeks, we gradually build up the distance we walk to 7 miles, we have found a new hobby and are enjoying exploring the local footpaths, discovering things that although having lived in the area all our lives we never knew existed. The thrill of turning a corner and coming across a long-forgotten building and wondering who built it and why, we are smugly proud of ourselves, they say that pride comes before a fall. Now that we are experienced walkers, we decide to walk along a local disused railway line for 4 miles until it links to a riverside walk by which we can return to the carpark, a total distance of around 7 miles. We set off, enjoying our new found hobby. After 3 hours or so we are both flagging a bit but we are nearing the carpark, so that's ok. Unfortunately, when we arrive, we discover that we are on the wrong side of the river and with no means of crossing it, we are ill prepared for the situation with no proper map only a print off from the internet. We are forced to extend our walk by an additional 4 miles to find a bridge in order to cross the river! By the time we arrive back at the car we have discovered two things, firstly to be better prepared and secondly what chafing is! Oh, how we laughed!

The Challenge Working Party continue to meet on a regular basis. We have split into sub-groups, in order to cover more ground and as the group had become so large that zoom meetings were starting to be problematic. Everyone is settling into their roles, and although progress is being made there seems to be an ever-growing list of tasks to be completed. I've been asked to produce a history of GDNF for use on leaflets and am currently trying to obtain information from the entrants regarding their challenges, such as team name, team members, contact details etc. And its proving to be troublesome, some entrants supplied the info immediately whilst others haven't even acknowledged the request. It worries me about their commitment.

It was announced at the last Working Party meeting that the writer and comedian Paul Mayhew Archer will be taking part in the challenge, previously he has donated the charity collection from his tour to Darren's fund and appears in the video for Vicki's song 'Shine'.

16th September 2020

Received an email from Jayne with news of a new study that is recruiting. 'PD SENSORS' is an exciting, new study which will look at how to measure aspects of Parkinson's and daily life using technological sensors. Alan Whone and his Movement Disorders team will be working closely with Computer Science Engineers from the University of Bristol in this pilot study.

The team are looking to recruit more pairs of participants, each pair containing one person with Parkinson's and one other person (e.g., someone within their social bubble) to come and stay in a terraced house in Bristol for 5 days. During this time, the participants will mostly continue to live as normal while being monitored by devices which include wrist-worn wearables.

The team are hoping to enhance the current methods of evaluating Parkinson's with a view to improving clinical trials looking for disease-modifying therapies in Parkinson's.

A quick word with Anna later and I'm emailing and phoning Cathy, the principal investigator, to express our interest in taking part.

Over the course of the next couple of weeks we are assessed for suitability for the study and we learn what it will entail for us. This is all via Zoom which has become the accepted way to interact with people during the ongoing Covid-19 pandemic. If this is a taste of the virtual world that beckons to us from the not-too-distant future then I don't like it, a world where you either can't or don't hug and kiss the people you love is a lesser place.

We are pleased to be accepted onto the study and agree a week in December when we can take our 'holiday.'

Good News

20th September 2020

Although it would appear that there has been little progress with GDNF, the Participants Working Party have continued working tirelessly to keep hopes of further research alive. It would appear that this pressure is finally beginning to work, Parkinson's UK have come up with a proposal which they wish to share with the group.

It's unusual for Parkinson's UK to ask to meet with us so it could be that there has been some form of progress. A defining moment in our campaign.

We need to illustrate the continued commitment within the group, and so it is vitally important that we have as many participants as possible attending. A show of strength now, to demonstrate our belief that GDNF actually works, will possibly be enough to tip the balance in our favour.

16.00 23rd September 2020

The group have responded well and there is a constant hum as participants who have not spoken to each other for a while catch up. My eyes move backwards and forward across the computer screen scanning the familiar faces, they all have the same hopeful look, I hope that we are not going to be disappointed.

The meeting is called to order by S from Parkinson's UK, who thanks us for attending and for our continued support. He announces that Parkinson's UK still see the potential of GDNF and other Neurotrophic factors, but there are outstanding questions that need to be answered. However, there are also complex challenges that need to be overcome in order to take GDNF forwards, and they have a 3-stage plan to unlock the current stalemate and move onwards.

I'm impressed, and I pinch myself in case it's just a dream, but I am wide awake and it hurts.

He warns us that what we are about to hear is strictly confidential and for the moment we cannot share or discuss anything we hear today. He introduces A, who begins to fill in the details.

Stage 1

There is to be a period of between 3 - 6 months, to determine if the outstanding challenges which currently prevent GDNF from moving forwards can be overcome.

If stage 1 is successful, they will move onto stages 2 and 3.

I quickly scan the screen; a rare thing has happened the GDNFer's have been stunned into silence.

Stage 2

A further period of between 12 – 24 months to carry out negotiations with the regulators, suppliers, investors and potential partners to formulate a plan to deliver a new clinical trial of GDNF, including securing funding.

Stage 3

A new phase 2 clinical trial of GDNF.

We are warned that if any stage is not successful, they will be unable to move onto the next stage and the whole process will halt. This is the best news that the group have ever received and although a new trial is still a long way away, with many hurdles to leap and boxes to tick, it is a way forward.

Thank you, Parkinson's UK.

The meeting closes with a request for volunteers, either trial participants or their partners, to join a focus group which will use their trial experiences to provide feedback on specific issues for stage 1. I watch as the individual zoom boxes slowly close down on the screen, most people are, I think, to stunned for much idle conversation, I certainly am. Anna, who has been sat beside me throughout the whole meeting sums it all up when she turns to me and says.

'Wonderful

Lots Of Updates

17th November 2020

I have just sent an email to all of the
Challenge entrants inviting them to an
update Zoom meeting. There has been
a great deal of progress made in the
planning for the event and the working
party want to bring all of the entrants
together not only to pass on this
information but also to make the
entrants feel more involved, and
thereby start to build a sense of unity
between the teams, after all it is a
unifying challenge.

A date has been set for 24th November
@7.00 p.m.

I also take the opportunity to gently
remind the entrants of my recent
request for information from them.

There are several people who after initially agreeing to take part, do not respond to any of my emails. I am slightly concerned.

Paul Mayhew Archer gets in touch, unfortunately he has a clash of commitments and can no longer take part in the challenge. He has been given the likely schedule for the shooting of a film he has written and it is in early April and early May.

This is obviously a big disappointment to lose our celebrity entrant, but he sweetens the blow by offering to attend the celebration party that is being planned for after the challenge and perform some comedy for us. What a generous offer.

21st November 2020

The group, via Jayne, receive an update on Parkinson's UK's investigation into the feasibility of a new GDNF trial.

Since we met with Parkinson's UK over £200,000 has been spent hiring a specialist consultancy who have been working on four specific areas for a new GDNF trial;

Legal

The Device

Scientific

Financing

These areas have been thoroughly investigated and the findings presented to the Board of trustees on 20th November. The outcome of the Stage 1 investigation is now in the hands of the trustees, who will make the decision as to whether to move forward to Stage 2.

The board are due to meet on 2nd December and the group will be informed within 7 days of their decision, with a full explanation of the reasoning behind this. I know that the Working Party have given 110% to ensure that it will be a positive decision.

Originally Parkinson's UK did not want them to have the opportunity to put their reasons for wanting a new trial to the Board of Trustees. And they had to fight long and hard before Parkinson's UK agreed to let them submit a short statement.

However, the Working Party turned the short statement into a video presentation, it was powerful and explained their belief in GDNF and their reasons for continuing to pursue it

We can do no more except wait and see. It's going to be a tense few weeks.

24th November 2020

Its 7.00p.m. and the Challenge update meeting has just begun, Jayne is telling us all that the charities have eventually agreed on the concept and wording for the Challenge, or as we should be calling it 'GDNF Participant's Unifying Challenge – In Support of Neurotrophic Factors.' It has taken a lot of work. Cure Parkinson's in particular were adamant that 'GDNF' should not be part of the name. Discussions have been protracted with Jayne and Lesley insisting that 'GDNF' is the central reason why the challenge is in existence and so should be part of the name. After all the idea had been entirely ours, we are doing all the work. We are not prepared to lose our identity and if necessary, will go it alone. After much debate the adding of 'neurotrophic factors' to the name has been deemed acceptable and here we are, all working together.

This is indeed fantastic news.

As entrants sign up to the Challenge, they will be able to choose which of the charities to fund raise for, with the proceeds being directed to their next Neurotrophic Factor project.

The entrants will need to set up a 'Just Giving' page for each team, which they should personalise with their stories, how they are linked to GDNF, details of their challenge and a few photos. It is planned that there will be an interactive map on the website which will have links directing the viewer to the 'Just Giving' pages. The meeting finishes with a slide presentation which acts as a reminder of all the finalised items to date. The meeting has been a great success and I believe that those who have attended are firmly hooked and committed to the challenge. The problem is that out of a possible 38 teams who have signed up to date, only 23 were in attendance tonight.

There are only approximately 6 weeks until we launch the Challenge on the 14th January, including Christmas. Then a frighteningly short 12 weeks until the event, we need all details finalised and the entrants confirmed. Before we run out of time.

7th December 2020

We receive a short message from Parkinson's UK. The Board of Trustees have asked for some additional information and their decision will now be announced by the end of January

2021. This is actually good news and demonstrates that they are taking the proposal seriously and giving it due consideration.

The LEARN Study

Listening to the Experience

of pARticipants in Neurosurgical trials

28th November 2022

I receive an email from Vicki, one of our leading lights in the GDNF Participants Working Party. She has been approached by two researchers from Cardiff University, Emma and Cheney, they are setting up a study which is being funded by Parkinson's UK, but is independent. They would like the Working Party's input and to utilise their experiences to help formulate the study protocol and design.

The aim is to understand how participation in clinical trials affects the daily life of those taking part and their partners. Thereby improving future Neurosurgical trials and to give future participants a better trial experience than we received, to that end they would like to interview as many of the GDNF participants and their partners as possible.

Vicki goes on to say that she has already met with them and is clearly impressed, it will mean extra work for us all but will be an amazing opportunity to tell our story. In the meantime, she has attached a list of questions and probes that they would like us to look at and ascertain whether or not the answers would capture our stories sufficiently? Is there any jargon? Have they missed anything? Is there anything we want added?

Clinical trials must be like buses, you wait for ages and then 3 turn up all at once.

A date is set for the first Zoom meeting, unfortunately its going to be early afternoon. So, I email Emma to make my excuses as I will still be at work. I receive a reply to say that they will try to arrange future meetings to better suit me, she continues to say that she had been hoping to speak with me as she has read my book and found it incredibly insightful. She would love to have me participate as an interviewee of course but also wondered if I would give my permission for my book to be used as additional evidence? They had found it useful in terms of constructing a timeline.

I'm flattered, to think a respected Neurological researcher enjoyed my book. Wow.

I reply, thanking her for her kind words. And telling her that I am more than happy to give permission for them to use my book in relation to the study.

Several Zoom meetings have been set up to allow the 'LEARN' team to pick what is left of our brains and gather our thoughts on the proposed questions and probes that have been produced. They certainly know how to ask a question in order to maximise the response, and the conversation flows amongst us. I am hearing about everyone's personal journeys through the trial. Shocking in parts, but also brutally honest and so detailed. This is the priceless information that wasn't wanted during the trial, but will now be captured. If what's been said during these sessions is representative of the rest of the participants, then Emma and Cheney are going to be busy.

The 'LEARN' study has now been announced to the group at large. They are told that it's on target to start interviewing the participants sometime next year after all the required approvals have been obtained. It is hoped that all of the participants will be able to contribute to this valuable study. Using the questions and probes that we help to devise they will be taken back to before the beginning of the trial, to hopefully remember their feelings, hopes and concerns throughout and after the trial and especially what they would like to see

happen differently to improve new
trials from a patient's perspective.

The Big Brother (Sphere) House

Monday 7th December 2020, or as it is now going to be known as;

Day number 1 in the 'Big Brother House', start day for the PD SENSORS study, it will also turn out to be 'The day the music died' for me.

Anna and I pack our suitcases for our 'holiday', we discuss the need for swimming costumes but on balance decide not to take them as there is no beach and if there was a swimming pool, then ice skates would be more appropriate given the weather.

We are due to meet with Cathy at 11.00a.m. in the 'Sphere House'. This is a house owned by Bristol University that has been rigged full of sensors and cameras which will inter-react with the

83

sensors that we shall both be wearing to provide a snap shot of 5 days in my life, symptom wise, with Anna providing the control. The data that this will produce will then be used to help develop a more accurate method of recording the impact that Parkinson's has. These tools could then be used during future trials to monitor participants in their own homes, at their best and worst 24/7.

We arrive slightly late and block the road whilst we unpack the car, I then go in search of a parking space. When I return Cathy welcomes us warmly and gives us a tour of the house together with a 'do's and don'ts' talk. The house itself is a Victorian terrace with 2 bedrooms, looks comfortable and is furnished to a good holiday let standard, the only thing missing is the usual broken bucket and spade that has been left by a previous tenant. Looking around you can't fail to notice that there are dozens of small electronic boxes everywhere, all linked by a spaghetti junction of wires, I think it must be what the human body would look like turned inside out with all the nerves, veins etc. on show.

We are reminded that there are different types of cameras being used some of which record shapes or outlines only, these are on 24/7 and colour video cameras these are on for 2 hours a day at a time requested by ourselves. There are no cameras upstairs, this is a relief not only for me but for the world at large, which I don't think is ready to see my slightly less than perfect body starring in some sort of Parkinson's porn.

Cathy carries out an on medication UPDRS assessment on both of us and we 'carry out scripted activities' this consists of buttering some bread, slicing bananas and making milk shakes. We are then left to settle in. Starting at 6.00 p.m. we have to keep a diary at 30-minute intervals recording medication taken, activities, symptoms and so on. We make some tea and then the music dies.

Cathy texts me my 'on' medication UPDRS from today's assessment 29!

I am shocked, the last time I was assessed it was off medication and I scored 19 and that was only 15 months ago. This confirms what I have really known for a few months but didn't want to admit, the GDNF magic is wearing off! At first, I had thought that at the age of 57 I had started to grow again, this was 2-fold. I had noticed an increasing difficulty 'slipping' my coat on, often ending up with my arms tangled behind my back in my coat which had somehow turned into a strait jacket. Also, when getting in and out of the car I had grown so much that my head and legs would not fit through the door, sadly it was really my body stiffening up as 'Mr Parkinson's' slowly returned, stamping the GDNF into submission. Later in the week is an 'off' medication assessment, that's going to be interesting.

Day number 2 in the 'Big Brother House'.

Tuesday, today is a 'free living 'day, this means that we can do as we please with no assessments we only have the diaries to complete every 30 minutes. I'm up at my usual time, 4.30 to 5.00

a.m. Every night I set my alarm for 6.00 a.m. in the hope that it will wake me up. Only to find myself waking in agony, hours early because my back has decided it's time to get up. The up side of this is I can start completing my diary nice and early, the down side is that I have more entries to complete. Anna wakes at a more reasonable 8.30 to 9.00 a.m. and we busy ourselves doing nothing. Around midday we decide to do some dance practice the problem being, where? We decide on the dining room so I move the chairs and table to one side. We manage a Jive and a Rumba but space constraints mean no Waltz, Foxtrot or Quickstep.

In the afternoon we spend an hour or so going for a walk, exploring the neighbourhood. The house is situated on Bristol University campus and as we stroll around, we notice that in most streets the majority of houses are in fact University buildings, we wonder at the value of their property assets when most of these houses would be worth in the region of a million pounds each. We return to the house and play a game of scrabble. We spend the evening catching up with our diaries.

Day number 3 in the 'Big Brother House'

Another 'Free living' day which turns out to be a carbon copy of the previous day. I'm taking things a bit easier as I have started to come off medication in readiness for tomorrow's assessment. I start by stopping any long-acting medication the day before the assessment and then not taking any other Parkinson's medication after 6.00 p.m. This means that by the time I carry out the assessment I have not taken some of my medication for over 24 hours. I have done this several times during the trial and since without too much trouble.

We retire to bed at around 11.00 p.m., I am tired and yet somehow cannot sleep and then it starts. It begins with a buzzing sensation in my knees and develops into an ache and then a twitch, restless leg syndrome, a new gift for me from 'Mr Parkinson's'. I cannot sleep so I get up, wander around, have a drink and try to sleep again. I am just drifting off when my legs twitch and I'm wide awake again. This happens several times and it is now getting late or is it early? Eventually I drift off, it's after 3.00 a.m. I have propped my knees up with some pillows and the weight of my legs hanging seems to reduce the twitch.

Day number 4 in the 'Big Brother House'

It's nice in life to have some things you can rely on; it's 4.30 a.m. and my back has kindly woken me. I have to get up due to the pain in my back.

I am completely exhausted, totally off medication, have hardly slept and its assessment day. We have agreed that Cathy is to come in early at 8.00 a.m. so I can be back on medication as soon as possible.

Cathy is prompt, she asks me how I'm feeling so I tell her of my overnight adventures and she apologises even though it's not her fault. We make a start as she is keen to get me back on medication as soon as possible.

It's the same UPDRS assessment as we completed on Monday, but this time I'm off medication and I know it. We repeat a couple of items when I think I can do better. After roughly 30 minutes we have finished and it's a cup of tea and a larger than normal dose of medication to return me to a blissfully drugged state, this takes about an hour or so, as slowly my head clears. We then repeat the assessment on medication and carry out the scripted activities again.

Cathy gives me my scores, on medication 26, so that's an improvement compared with Monday's assessment of 29. She explains that the assessment captures a moment in time and so can vary depending on all sorts of things.

She hesitates before telling me my off-medication score, 39. I was expecting something similar but when spoken aloud it seems worse.

I think back to my first ever UPDRS assessment, this was over 5 years ago in 2015 as part of the preparation for the trial and my score then was 42. If you add on the average 2-points progression for Parkinson's per year, you could realistically expect my score to be in the mid 50's, so I am still ahead of the game, at the moment.

Day number 5 in the 'Big Brother House' Friday, this is our last day, the diaries finish at 9.00 a.m. for which I'm thankful. The requirement to complete an entry every 30 minutes, although obviously important to help make sense of the hours and hours of video footage, has been a chore.

Cathy arrives at about 10.00 a.m. and removes the monitoring devices that we've been wearing since Monday. The sense of freedom this gives is remarkable and similar I Imagine to an ASBO recipient having their ankle tag removed. We are then debriefed and Cathy goes through our stay asking for any comments or suggestions that we may have to improve the experience for future participants. The conversation moves onto how the Sphere house has changed Cathy's perspective on how Parkinson's affects patients, how her eyes had been opened to the variation and severity of symptoms even after several years examining patients in a clinic setting. And then it's over, Cathy thanks us for our involvement and promises to send us a copy of the study report when it's ready. She cautions us that it may be a while as she has to go through all the video footage, diaries etc. and make some sort of sense of it not only for us but also the other participants as well.

It really has been a pleasure and I have a feeling of achieving something worthwhile. 5 days of our time is a small sacrifice to make if it helps towards the development of more accurate assessment tools for future trials.

A Launch & An Adjournment

1st January 2021

The Christmas holidays are just about over and what a strange Christmas it's been, due to the Covid 19 restrictions socialising has been virtually impossible. We usually host a Christmas Eve family carol singalong at our home, which is a great way to welcome Christmas. This year we held it by Zoom, which set the tone for the rest of the festivities, which I think we can sum up as   although fun, it wasn't the same.

Anyway, it's now a New Year and time for the Challenge is running short.

There are now only 89 days before the Challenge starts, so we have a limited time to achieve everything that needs to be in place by 1st April. The hard launch is set for 14th January and I am still awaiting some registration forms. We desperately need the information held on these missing forms as we are working on a virtual 'Challenge Map' which will show the location of all the teams challenges along with all their details, we would like to be able to go live with this for the launch, the map will be available on the Challenge website.

The website is going to be the hub of information for all things Challenge related and our point of contact with the world at large, giving access for donations to be made. We want to bring the teams to life, to help with this it would be nice to add photos of the teams undertaking their training and background information.

On launch day we want to obtain as much publicity as possible, we have produced a press release which we have sent to the entrants with the intention that they will send it on to their local media, tv, press, radio and any other interested parties.

I have reminded the entrants to ensure that they have set up their 'Just Giving' pages and to link it on to the team page. So, when friends or relatives visit either the website or 'Just Giving' they will be able to navigate to the various teams to make a donation.

Well, launch day has come and gone, and apart from an announcement on Parkinson's UK website. I have not seen or heard any mention of the challenge, it's almost as if radio silence has been declared. This is very disappointing, but apparently news editors are only interested in events that are current or happening. There is a limited amount of column inches and that's for today's news. Not something that's happening in tenweek's.

I think of all the effort that the Working Party have put into getting things ready for today, there must be some way to publicise the challenge? I remember the post that I put on Facebook when my book was first published, I compose a brief statement giving details of the Challenge and adding a link to my 'Just Giving' page as an afterthought.

A week later and I'm posting on Facebook again;

Hello,

Firstly, I would like to thank all of you who have donated to my 'GDNF Participants Unifying Challenge' Just

Giving page. I have been overwhelmed by your generosity you are most kind. As part of our challenge, we are dancing, the reason for this is because without GDNF there would be no dancing. Before the trial I would come home from work and simply go to sleep until I went to work again. After the trial Anna and I attended up to 3 dance classes every week as well as going to monthly dances and dance weekends. This is just one of the many ways GDNF improved not only my life but the life of our family. I have added a video of us recently practicing for the challenge, you can make your own mind up about whether the powers of GDNF are good or bad once you've seen us dancing, regardless of what you think of the dancing please donate to give other people the same chance that I had. Thank you.

People seem to like what I'm posting, friends and family are giving but I'm also getting donations of £10, £20 or £50 from complete strangers. Some have heard the GDNF story, others are new to it and request more details. Which I am more than happy to supply. The one thing they all have in common is the hope of a cure and as far as they can tell, GDNF is the best option.

1st February 2021

Received an email today from 'Just Giving' to say that my page for the GDNF Participants Unifying Challenge was one of the most successful, out of 1000's of fundraiser's, I was in the top 20%....I can take no credit for this myself as it is all down to the generosity of all the kind donors. Aren't people wonderful.

13th February 2021

There is a Working Party meeting tonight and the subject of Covid 19 was raised. At the moment the pandemic is ongoing with no real sign of the restrictions being lifted or reduced for the foreseeable future. Bearing in mind that several of our entrants will have to travel and use hotels or guest houses to carry out their challenges, it is being proposed that we delay the Challenge until there is some form of improvement in the Covid 19 restrictions.

A lively debate ensues. As it is I have my concerns about some entrant's commitment and think that a postponement may result in some teams pulling out. I ask if it would be possible for those teams who could complete their challenges within the current restrictions do so, with the remaining teams 'catching up' at some point later. We've been discussing the merits of all arguments, for and against a postponement when Jayne calls for a vote. We go around the room, when it's my turn I vote against a postponement but I'm the only one. Overall, it's the best way forwards and the dates are revised to 1st – 14th September for the actual Challenge with the celebration being the weekend of 2nd – 3rd October.

On the plus side it gives us more time to make it perfect, on the minus side we will have to keep the entrants interested for longer.

I am disappointed, people need an end point, they cannot give on a never-ending basis. However, I can see the reasoning behind the postponement. Hopefully the Covid 19 restrictions will either be reduced or maybe even lifted altogether and agree that this is the only way to move on if it's to be truly unifying, with all the teams completing their challenges at the same time. My other concern is the monies raised so far, people have donated in good faith to help enable further studies into Neurotrophic Factors, but they will still understandably want the challenge to take place. And we've just postponed it for 5 months. We have to keep both the entrants and the public interested and give them value for their money.

I've been mulling things over for a In recognition of the faith people have bestowed upon the Challenge and the hope it gives for the future, I have set myself an additional personal challenge.

Dancing was always going to play a small part in my Challenge. Together with my lovely wife Anna we will attempt to cover an additional 100 miles by dancing. This will take place between the original Challenge start date 1st April and the new start date 1st September, a period of 22 weeks, during our practice sessions we usually manage around 2 - 2.5 miles between us every week. So, as you can see it will be a challenge.

Good News & A Return To Form

22nd February 2021

The Participant group receives a message from Parkinson's UK which they felt was imperative for us to have prior to their public announcement.

Following the group's meeting with them on 23rd September, when they announced the review of their plans for the future of GDNF. This was completed in November and along with the recommendations, including the group's contribution, was submitted to the Board of Trustees for approval. Well today, the Board have announced their approval of the charity's plans to take the next step towards developing a new clinical trial of GDNF.

Parkinson's UK are planning to invest up to £800,000 over the next 1-2 years to create a robust new study that meets the needs of patients, regulatory agencies and investors. A new company has been created to drive forward the planning and preparations for a new trial. Crucially, this new company will receive all the data and intellectual property associated with GDNF from Med-Genesis. If this work is successful, a new trial could start in 2022. Parkinson's UK continue to say that we must also recognise that the ultimate result may be that a further trial will not be possible, and that we must look to other approaches to deliver Neurotrophic Factors to the brain.

The inspiration and successful outcome of this review has been achieved through the joint endeavours of

Parkinson's UK and the GDNF Participant Group Working Party, who have both worked tirelessly to keep GDNF research alive. We want to say a heartfelt thank you to everyone involved in the previous trial. Without your courage and dedication, we would not be where we are today.

Parkinson's UK will be formally announcing this news in the media and on their website at 9.00am tomorrow 23rd February. Until then, they request that we do not share or discuss this news with anyone outside the GDNF Participant Group.

This is fabulous news and a real step forward. I'm beginning to think that a new trial may, possibly, perhaps, perchance, conceivably, feasibly take place. The next day at just after 9.00am I'm on Parkinson's UK's website searching for any more details, unfortunately they also release a Press statement.

I glance through the statement, stop and start to read it properly. I cannot believe the arrangement of words in front of me. This is a real slap in the face for the Participant's Group and in particularly for the Working Party. 5 people who for the last 4 or so years have given up days and days of their time to ensure that GDNF does not get forgotten about. And yet they have been forgotten about with a few words.

How can Parkinson's UK treat the group with such insensitivity?

The statement begins.

'Our ground breaking clinical trial….'.

The trial was a partnership of many organisations including The Cure

Parkinson's Trust, Med-genesis, Funding Neuro, Renishaw and many more. If it was anyone's trial then that should be The North Bristol NHS Trust who organised, ran and hosted it. Certainly not Parkinson's UK. If it was their trial, in that case why did they refuse initially and only later reluctantly supply any form of aftercare for the participants?

The statement continues.

'We believe in GDNF's potential. Some participants have told us they're still experiencing the benefits, years on from undergoing this experimental therapy. We want to make sure we've explored every option.'

I'm sorry but there is only one word to describe that sentence, BULLSHIT!

When I realised that I was still improving a year or so after my last infusion, I thought that the information stored within my body was so important that I should at least be seen or hopefully assessed to capture what was happening. After all who knows where the key to a cure lies.

Over several weeks I attempted to speak to someone at Parkinson's UK about this. My emails went unanswered or were bounced around several members of staff. Eventually in an attempt to rid themselves of me, I had a phone conference with A from the research department and his assistant, we had a long conversation regarding the merits of assessing me, which ended with me, very nicely, being told to go away and not return.

'You are of no scientific interest.' Was the term used.

They certainly didn't 'explore every option.'

Apparently, they have also.

'Learnt from the previous trial, and will be putting the wellbeing of the participants at the centre of any new trial.'

I hope that this is true because they have never even considered our wellbeing and every tiny step that they have made towards helping us has had to be dragged out of them. We were treated as a commodity, to be used and then abandoned.

The press statement gives the impression that Parkinson's UK have been championing GDNF and doing everything in its power to ensure another trial takes place. Until recently the truth is that since the trial failed, they have been distancing as far as possible from any negative fallout the failure may have caused.

The Participant's Group is mentioned in passing but not named even though without the group GDNF would have been long forgotten, deemed a failure, consigned to history as a waste of time.

Parkinson's UK's whole attitude towards us and 'The ground breaking new treatment' has only really changed since Gary has been involved and I suspect that their warming towards us is under his influence and whoever drafted the press statement must, surely, have been old school.

We have always had a tempestuous relationship with Parkinson's UK. During the trial most participants knew

that Parkinson's UK were one of the
sponsors and towards the end of the
trial we were gradually introduced to
various people who worked for them
and a relationship of sorts was formed,
these people became the business face
of the trial for many of the participants.

When the trial ended and we were
looking for support we turned to
Parkinson's UK. Unfortunately,
aftercare had not been included in the
trial design, this was a major mistake
but not necessary Parkinson's UK's
fault. Remember this was a ground
breaking trial the likes of which had
never been seen before, usually when a
trial ends that's it stop taking the
medication, thank you and goodbye.

Yet here we are an elite group of
people who all had experimental
devices in their brains, that 99.9% of all

doctors and nurses had never even seen. Despite this they were being expected to deal with any problems that emerged, no one had considered what was going to happen to the Participants.

In our early conversations with Parkinson's UK, with hindsight, I think we were blaming them for all the mistakes in the trial and that wasn't fair. In return I think we panicked them with our demands. There were faults on both sides.

However, over the course of the intervening years a mutual respect has been formed, after all we all want the same thing and are working together to achieve it. It has taken a long time to gain each other's trust and to appreciate the work that is going on behind the scenes and the particular difficulties in moving on from a failed trial.

We now work well together; we understand each other's point of view. Yes, we still, sometimes, have differences but we can resolve them.

You may think from the tone of this book that our relationship is poor; this may be true at the start. However, without trying they have grown in my estimation and their actions have earnt my respect.   The events related in this book are truthful but from my viewpoint, so please bear this in mind. Parkinson's UK do a lot of good works for the Parkinson's community, which we should be grateful for. Also, we must remember that having sampled the benefits of GDNF we have tunnel vision on that subject, all we think about is GDNF whereas To Parkinson's

UK GDNF is only one of many research projects they are running and who knows which one will eventually result in a cure.

We just hope that Parkinson's UK really are 100% behind GDNF.

I sit and consider the recent warming in the relationship between us and what we could possibly achieve if we continue to work together. At best the press release is poorly worded, at worst it is insulting. However, at the same time, without the commitment and the innovation of the Parkinson's UK team who conceived and negotiated a deal with Med-genesis the prospect of a trial would still be remote.

In my head I take a step backwards and weigh up the facts, a new trial for GDNF would be a dream come true for the group and we are closer now than ever before. If you compare this against having to swallow your pride there is no contest. If Parkinson's UK need to air brush the last 4 years in order for GDNF to move forward then that is a price I am willing to pay, but it does not mean I like it.

The Challenges

1st April 2021

I don't know if the date is a message from above, but today is the first day of our 100-mile dance challenge. We are both working for the rest of the week so our first dance session will have to wait until Sunday. We have been encountering problems trying to accurately measure the distance covered, after practice sessions we have had varied results ranging from 0.2 - 2 miles using a standard pedometer. I think it must be missing all the side steps and turns. We've looked into specialist dance pedometers without any success and even Google fails to find anything suitable. After much thought and based on the assumption that beats roughly

119

equal steps per minute, we have come up with the following;

Beats / steps per minute

Multiplied by

Duration of music in minutes

Equals

Total steps per piece of music

Multiplied by

Average step length in metres

Divide by

1609.34 (number of metres in a mile)

Equals

Distance covered in miles

We've probably devised the most complicated method for attempting to measure distance since logarithms were invented. One day the world will thank us, but not today.

6th April 2021

Emma from the 'LEARN' study gets in touch, they have now obtained all of the required permissions and approvals and are keen to speak to as many participants and loved ones as possible to get a full understanding of the trial experience. We will be invited to take part in Zoom or telephone interviews to share our experiences and thoughts about the GDNF trial.

The Challenge Working Party are keen to try and maintain the entrants drive and determination over the next few months until the delayed start date of 1st September. There is a hardcore of perhaps 30 entrants who are very committed to the challenge, attend all

121

the meetings, and have complied with any requests that we've made of them. Then there's the others who I'm calling the ghost entrants, you're not sure if they exist but sometimes you can feel a presence.

We don't want to lose anyone, so we must keep them interested. Team highlights have been suggested, each team would produce a short biography. Who they are? Their connection to GDNF? Why they decided to take part in the challenge. With maybe a few photos, all of which could be sent out to all the teams by email and updated on the website, on the basis of 1 team highlighted each week which should cover the 20 or so weeks until the challenge begins, hopefully, it will build a sense of community, with like-minded people bonding together.

We also release details for the Challenge celebration, because after all everyone loves a party.

In celebration of the presumed successful completion of the Unifying Challenge, the Working Party are planning a re-union for all GDNF Trial Participants and also a Dinner Dance for Trial Participants and Challenge Entrants. The venue is to be 'The Bristol Hotel,' Prince Street, Bristol. with the Dinner Dance being held on Saturday 2nd October and the re-union on Sunday 3rd October.

Costings will be finalised soon and Parkinson's UK have kindly offered to subsidise some of the expense for the Trial Participants and partners. This is a very generous gesture by Parkinson's UK and it will enable as many participants as possible to attend, which is great news. It's going to be a spectacular and we don't want anyone to miss out, so we ask the entrants for an indication of their intentions to attend or not.

26th April 2021

I have just updated the Working Party on interest for the celebration. We have 27 confirmed guests for the dinner dance, comprising all the usual suspects, most of which will also be staying over for the re-union the following day. So, that's an excellent start.

I then move on to update the Working Party on the response for the Team highlights. If I say interest has been slow then I mean that I have received no replies at all. In the absence of any other highlights, I produce one for my team A.K.A. 'The Retreaters', named after our house, and add a request for other teams to send in theirs. Although I don't think I'm going to be swamped by the deluge, I will put on my metaphysical wellies just in case.

Let's hope I am wrong.

3rd May 2021

It's now roughly 5 weeks into our 100-mile dance challenge and despite me struggling to move my feet yesterday morning, we have now covered 29.75 miles. So we are on target, and our dance classes start again next week which will add a bit to the total.

Over the first couple of weeks, I videoed us dancing and posted it on Facebook in case anyone was interested. We now have 'Dance Cam', this is a video of us dancing viewed from my field of vision, so all you see is the walls of the room we are in and various parts of Anna's arms, head etc. moving as we perform different types of dances. Oh, and I've muted the sound so you can't hear the music. I then ask if anyone can identify what dance we are doing, this has been quite popular. The first time was the Jive which several people correctly identified, this was reassuring that people could actually recognise what we were doing.

Since then, Dance Cam has been out capturing a dancer's eye view of the Rumba, Waltz, Foxtrot, Tango and so on, sometimes no one guesses correctly. When this happens, we are a little concerned in case we are doing it completely wrong.

18th May 2021

Here we are day 47 out of 153 of our 100-mile Dance Challenge and I'm pleased to announce that the running total is 42.03 miles. We are officially ahead of target, I must thank my understanding dance partner and wife, Anna, and my legs for doing as they are told over the last couple of weeks.

21st May 2022

There is still the on-going saga of obtaining details of their challenges from the 'ghosts', I don't think there's a problem, they will do the Challenge but not the paperwork. I was talking to Anna about it and she suggested that I contact them again.

She said;

'Who you gonna call?'

I reply.

'Ghost busters.'

Planning for the challenge itself is well advanced. The highlights have been arriving regularly and we now have enough to last nearly until the Challenge starts, they make interesting reading with the recurring theme being remarkable, determined people doing extraordinary things in the pursuit of a cure. I feel fortunate to be part of it.

The charities have agreed to provide promotional hats, t-shirts etc for the entrants supporting them. And are busy imparting their knowledge and expertise regarding the practicalities of fund raising.

Plans for the Celebration are shaping up nicely, we have set up a sub-party to deal purely with the celebration, we currently have 18 rooms allocated and 44 guests booked for the dinner dance on the Saturday evening. This will include a 3-course meal, Comedian Paul Mayhew Archer has promised to provide some entertainment and there will be speeches. We will then enjoy music and be able to dance the night away. We would love this to be an event where everyone can dress up and make the most of being, hopefully, released from our Covid 19 shackles.

On the Sunday morning after breakfast, we will have a closed meeting for all Participants and their partners, hopefully Parkinson's UK will attend and will be able to give us an update on the progress of the new trial. We should finish around mid-day.

16th June 2021

Jayne has invited me to join the GDNF Working Party, it's nice to be asked and I accept. I have thoroughly enjoyed working on the challenge and will miss the cut and thrust of menu choices and room allocation when it finishes. When all of this challenge started, I didn't know what to expect or if I would be of any use, it just proves that you should try new experiences occasional.

7th July 2021

There are just 56 days left to complete our '100-Miles Dance Challenge'

The good news is that despite several sessions which finished after only 10 - 15 minutes due to what we call 'my sticky feet', this is when it seems that I have stood in a large pool of super glue and no matter how much I try I just cannot move.

To date we have had 34 sessions with the mileage ranging from a few yards to a personal best for us of 6.6 miles. We have actually covered 85 miles, leaving just 15 miles to go. Which we are hoping to complete over the next few weeks. Leaving us a short time to prepare for the main event.

9th July 2021

Parkinson's UK have been listening to us it appears; they are setting up the GDNF Involvement Advisory Board and have invited 3 of our most valued members to join. Jayne, Lesley and Nic. Their mission, should they decide to accept it, is to represent the Participant Group's viewpoint on the Board and to advise on trial aspects from a participant's perspective. They will be working in conjunction with Parkinson's UK and the Patient and Public Involvement group. This is a real opportunity to be in the front line and to have a say in the evolution of a new trial.

14th August 2021

I am pleased to announce that Anna and I have now completed our 100-miles dance challenge, 2 weeks early. In total we have had 37 sessions with an average of 2.7 miles danced per session, but of course life isn't average and the reality is that some days, when 'Mr Parkinson's' didn't want to play, we barely danced more than a few steps. On other glorious days the miles just flew by with us covering 5 – 6 miles. It was exhausting at times, but mostly it was simply fun and we enjoyed doing it.

1st September 2021

Today, is the first day of the 'The GDNF Participants' Unifying Challenge' which had been planned to take place in April this year but had to be postponed due to the Covid 19 restrictions. It's going to run from 1st – 14th September and promises to be an excellent example of what can be achieved when people work together with a common goal.

All over the country there are groups of people who are shaking, stumbling and sitting exhausted by the roadside after trying to walk, run, cycle or even dance a few miles. All to raise money for, and increase the public's awareness of Neurotrophic Factors, such as GDNF. This disease modifying treatment for Parkinson's must be given another chance to prove itself, the previous trial only failed due to poor trial design and the use of outdated assessment tools. If you ask any of the previous trial participants, they will tell you how GDNF changed their lives and gave them hope of a cure, not in 15 - 20 years, but soon. All of the details are on our website gdnf.org.uk Visit it to find out why a group of strangers have come together to try to change the scientific community's opinion about a treatment which they had consigned to the dust bin, and how that opinion is slowly changing. Check the amazing running total for the challenge and remember that a lot of the teams comprise of severely disabled people. The chances are that someone that you know and love either has Parkinson's or will have it. GDNF could be helping them.

For Anna and I our challenge will start on Saturday 4th September, when we have planned a pleasant walk with family and friends which we are going to repeat on the following Saturday with a different group.

We assemble just after 9.00am, there are 12 of us. I have planned a route of approximately 7 miles, with a shortcut home after 4.5 miles for the more infirm team members (me). It's a bright and sunny day, with a bit of cloud cover which will stop us getting burnt. We leave the house and cross the road onto a foot path that leads us down to the Frome Valley Walk, a lovely river side amble which alternates between a shady path on the riverbank and, as the river slowly meanders, open farmland.

We are taking our time, after all it's not a race we are there to enjoy the scenery and each other's company. The path crosses the river and we pass under a railway viaduct and then we immediately cross back over the river. At this point we take an intersecting pathway. And emerge onto a sleepy country lane which we follow until we have to cross a main road. The one group now becomes two as the old crocks, including me, taking the shorter route home over what until recently was farmland but has now become a building site.

The other half of the group continue across a golfclub, through some country lanes until they reach the railway again, this time crossing over it by means of a footbridge. They then return home, arriving literally 5 minutes after the old crocks, having walked an additional 2 miles.

It's time for refreshments, tea and coffee and a selection of cakes. There has obviously been a misunderstanding regarding numbers, as my mother who has kindly supplied the cakes and who only bakes in catering quantities has I think baked cakes for the entire Challenge, never mind there are worse problems than having a surplus of cakes. It's been a good day, and we get to repeat it next week.

Goodbye My Friend

9th September 2021

It's a Thursday evening, the challenge is well on its way and has, it seems, been a huge success, every day I get updates with incredible totals. It's working particularly from a unifying point of view; people are joining together with a common goal. It's so satisfying that all the work over the last 15 months has been so worthwhile.

I have just received an email from Mary, Jeff's wife, telling me of his amazing team total to date, 639 miles, with more to come. I sit back marvelling at Jeff's achievement as I do so I'm casually running my hand over what remains of my hair. My hand catches on something, I am suddenly aware that it is my port, the visible part of the drug delivery system installed within my brain, and something is wrong.

What had previously fitted close to the scalp is now protruding and sitting at a strange angle, there is a clear gap between it and my skin. The words concern and worry do not cover the emotions that I am experiencing, what has happened? What could be wrong? I ask Anna if she will take a look, she does so and asks for my phone, she wants to take a picture to show me. I look at it and can see a shadow around the edge of the port, this is the gap which shouldn't be there and the gap tapers showing that the port is now not in alignment. I think of the recent port problems that have been reported by other participants, those seemed to be infection related, what the hell has happened.

By now it's nearly 8.00p.m. what do I do?

It's out of hours, but I ring Alan, he answers on the 1st ring and I explain myself, he is reassuringly calm and listens intently as I relate what has happened. He tells me not to worry and that he will sort something out. An hour or so later he rings back, he has spoken to Neil from the Neuro Surgical team who will be ringing me the following morning. My port seems extremely loose and fragile, I'm concerned about sleeping on it so I sleep downstairs in a chair which has a back that is lower than the level of my port, this seems to work.

Around 8.45a.m. the following morning my mobile bursts into life leaving me with the usual Parkinson's struggle to press the correct button to connect the call before either the answering machine kicks in or I cancel the call altogether.

Neil, introduces himself and asks me to explain what's happened, he listens carefully, absorbing all the facts.

He makes an appointment for me to see the on-call registrar on a Neuro Surgical ward at 11.00a.m. On arrival, no space is available for me to be seen in so I'm seated in the corridor outside the ward and the registrar is called. He goes through the details with me and then asks if he can examine the port, he parts my hair and then exclaims a long protracted 'Ahhhhh'.

At that moment, I immediately know that he has never seen a port before and therefore cannot possibly know what he's looking for in terms of any problems. He decides to take a photo which is duly sent to Neil, without another word he's off, never to be seen again. I think he may have been on holiday the day that bedside manner was taught.

In the absence of being told to either stay or go I opt to stay, half an hour or so later I am approached by a man who introduces himself as Neil, we run through my story again and then he examines me, he says that the port is secure. However, as he has never seen my port before he can't definitely say if it has moved at all. He is concerned and recommends the removal of the entire system just to be safe.

Previously I would not have been keen to take this step, but for a long time now I have realized that the chances of me ever receiving GDNF again are extremely remote. If the new trial starts as proposed then it would be a minimum of maybe 8 -10 years before I could even apply for it on compassionate grounds and even then, there is no guarantee that it would happen, and by that time after what would be 10 to 15 years of inactivity, would my system be safe to use or even functional?

I made my decision for this scenario a while ago, so I agree with Neil's advice. He tells me that I could be admitted on Monday and possibly have the surgery on Tuesday. This really is being fast tracked.

We decide to cancel our planned second walk and will hopefully be able to reschedule it soon.

By Monday morning I am sure that the port is sticking out even more. So, I ring and leave a message for Neil, he returns my call within an hour and is very reassuring. He tells me.

'Keep your phone with you today, we are just waiting for a bed and then you can come in, expect a call at any moment.'

The day passes slowly and I am just about resigned that I will not be going in today, when my phone rings. It is the bed manager; they have a space for me. Can I get there as soon as possible? My bag is already packed so we get into the car and make our way over.

I am reminded of the day 6 and a half years ago when Anna and I made the same journey to have the delivery device installed. So much has changed in that time and yet remained the same. For all of our efforts a cure for Parkinson's is still 5 to 10 years away. It's so frustrating when you know that there is a disease modifying treatment which could be helping Parkinson's sufferers now and yet it is not available because of greed. The previous journey marked the beginning of hope for me, this one and its purpose marks the end of my personal GDNF journey.

This thought makes me more determined than ever that the group must build on the success of the challenge and keep the pressure on to ensure that GDNF and other Neurotrophic Factors are fully investigated and given every opportunity to prove their restorative properties.

We arrive on a busy ward just as the evening meal is being served, we are expected and are taken to my room to settle in, visiting time has already been and gone so Anna shouldn't really be in with me, but a blind eye is turned. Within 15 minutes a member of the Neuro Surgical team arrives and begins to take a case history, he has just about finished when Neil arrives and says to his colleague.

'I expect you are wondering what this is all about.'

Neil then starts to explain to him all about the GDNF trial, he gets to the bit about failing to meet the primary end point and I interrupt to tell them both of how I had improved by 71%, that my UPDRS score had gone from 42 to 14 and that most other participants had improved. I finish and there is a silence in the room for a moment, which is broken by Neil who goes through the plan for the following day. Nothing to eat or drink after 2.00 a.m. as he is hoping to start around 9.00 to 10.00 a.m. They leave, shortly after Anna and I say our goodbyes as it is going to be an early start. Due to the covid 19 restricted visiting times she can only come in for an hour a day, so we decide to save the hour for after the brain surgery has taken place. This, of course, means that we will not see each other again before the procedure and she is a little tearful as we say good night to each other. Sophie our daughter is going to be with her the next day and I'm reassured by that.

Any Old Iron

I am awake by 4.30a.m. Overnight there had been no alternative but to sleep with my head / port resting on the pillow, so I gingerly use my hand to examine my port. It has moved back into my skull, the pressure of resting my head on the pillow has pushed it back. I'm so glad that it will be gone today.

I sit quietly in bed for an hour going through the forthcoming day's events, I am happy with everything but keen to get started. The nurse comes in at 6.00a.m. and we deal with the medication and blood pressure side of things, no breakfast for me. I will be getting ready soon. At 7.30a.m. I ring Anna to speak before I'm called down.

It is now 11.20a.m. and two doctors from Neuro surgery have been to see me they asked if I had any questions to which I replied.

'When is it going to happen?'

They just smiled.

I'm on auto repeat, I play scrabble, look at my phone, look out the window at the same tree, pace the room and repeat. When the door opens and Lucy from the trial pops her head in.

'Hello,' she says 'How are you?'

I am really pleased to see her and her smile brightens the room, we chat about my situation and the upcoming Challenge Celebration, which she is attending. She tells me that she has seen Neil, he is sorry for the delay and will get to me as soon as he can. As she leaves, they are serving lunch, but not for me as I'm 'nil by mouth.'

13.29 I am just dozing off and the door bursts open and a nurse says.

'You need to get ready.'

'When.' I reply.

'NOW!!!!!' she says.

There is a porter from theatre waiting outside the door. I grab the gown that has been left for me and proceed into the shower room to change, after about 30 seconds the nurse is asking if I am ready yet, in the rush I cannot tie the gown properly so I just hold it round me, dive into the bed and pull the sheets over me and then we are off. The porter is propelling the bed through the hospital corridors as if he is James Hunt at Silverstone, the medi-rooms door opens and we take the chequered flag and I am left in the pits still tying the gown up.

After a few minutes I am joined by an anaesthetist who runs through the consent form with me and checks that we have an accord on today's activities. Neil appears around a corner; he apologises for the delay and asks if I have any final questions or concerns before we start. I am wheeled into the theatre and the anaesthetist inserts a cannula into the back of my hand, through which she is injecting some drugs, there is a slight stinging sensation in the back of my hand and then.........

Someone is calling my name.

'Andy, Andy! Andy!! Andy!!!'

I slowly open my eyes and realise that it's all over, I struggle to keep my eyes open, I'm half sitting half lying down on the bed and a nurse is talking to me, gradually I begin to understand what she is saying to me. She is introducing herself and telling me that she knows Anna, that she has spoken to Anna and told her that I am now in recovery. She offers me a drink, which I accept gratefully as my throat is so dry. I ask her the time? It's just after 5.00p.m.

Slowly, I am coming to my senses and as clarity gradually returns, I am aware that the most overriding sensation of all is the need to use the toilet. I pass this knowledge onto the nurse looking after me, she disappears for a few moments and then she presents me with a bottle to use, I am desperate to use it but cannot, no matter how hard I try I cannot perform in that way while sitting half upright in a bed.

She asks if it would be easier if I was standing, to see if gravity could help, I can definitely see that working and I predict a successful outcome, and so it is decided to get me standing alongside the bed. In preparation for this she starts to move the bed sheet that is covering me, upon seeing the pants that I left on when donning the gown in a vain attempt to preserve my modesty, she begins to ease them down. Regrettably, the combined effect of her pulling and my weight results in a parting of the seams to which she says.

'Oh, I'm ripping them.'

Unfortunately, and I'm blaming all the drugs in my system. I find myself in the strange situation where your mouth works without engaging the brain, and I hear myself uttering the least appropriate words for the circumstances, which were

'It's been a long time since a lady ripped my pants off.'

Fortunately, the nurse has switched her ears off.

Help arrives in the form of an additional two nurses. I am guided to my feet and we play the lift game, this is when all the players look in different directions and pretend that there isn't a middle-aged man, half asleep, filling up a disposable bottle with a strange look of satisfaction on his face, amongst them. The mission successfully completed, they lower me back onto the bed and I promptly fall asleep.

I am unbelievably tired and cannot keep my eyes open for more than a few seconds, I open my eyes and Neil is there telling me how well everything went, I open them again and he has gone, the next time and the bed is moving, making our way back to the ward. A few minutes after our arrival and Anna is in the doorway, she hugs me and we kiss, it's really good to see her, she is talking to me asking how I am but the conversation is very one sided. Anna has seen me, she is happy. So, we decide it would be better if she returns home, I promise to ring her in the morning.

A nurse asks if I would like anything to eat or drink, suddenly I am very hungry, nothing has passed my lips since I had tea at home the day before. Fortunately, the evening meal has just been served and a tray appears before me, I realise that this is the meal I had ordered this morning. Cold ham, boiled potatoes with a salad and vanilla sponge with custard. I start with the pudding and slowly work my way through all of it, it's absolutely delicious and I clear the plate. I settle down and drift off to sleep, later I am awoken by the nurse entering the room, I assume it is the morning and ready myself to receive my medication when this doesn't happen, I ask the time?

'Midnight.' is the reply.

I have been in a deep sleep and yet am still exhausted, the nurse leaves and sleep returns.

It's 7.30a.m. and I have just woken Anna up, in the two hours since I awoke the nurse has taken my blood pressure and temperature, shone a torch in my eyes, I've squeezed her hand, pushed my legs against her and taken my medication. Breakfast has been eaten and I'm washed and dressed, now I'm speaking to Anna and next I am planning on going back to sleep. I've had 12 hours solid sleep, 4 times what I normally get by on and yet I'm still exhausted, I must be getting old, no more recreational brain surgery for me if it makes you feel like this.

I spend the day dozing, playing solo scrabble and catching up on Challenge news, which ended yesterday and I missed it. Success is such an inadequate word to describe it and I can't think of a word that has the energy, power, camaraderie and collaboration to cover it. So, for the time being I shall call it a success. Around mid -morning Neil and his team call in; he is very concerned about how I am feeling and I ask if he found any problems with my port that may have been the cause of the movement.

He replies.

'No, nothing at all, in fact I had a job to remove it.'

He continues.

'Everything went very well; we will remove the bandage tomorrow and if it's healing nicely then you can go home.'

I'm just glad that the delivery system is safely out, I wonder what will happen to the metal work that I've carried around for over 6 years. I decide that Neil will probably put it out for recycling, and that once a week a horse and cart pulls into the hospital grounds, the driver leads his horse across the site to the dustbins behind the operating theatres, all the while shouting out.

'Any old iron, top prices paid, any old iron.'

Upon his arrival the driver rummages through the bins and then goes on his way delighted with his haul of a GDNF delivery port.

Anna arrives just as I am finishing lunch bringing with her a large hot chocolate with cream and marshmallows, it really is very nice so I suggest that we have one every day from now on, she gives me a scornful look and says,

'Next time you will be in the Bariatric unit.'

I smile at her as I think it would be a good night out to see the Welsh headwear juggler in action.

16th September, the following morning, I have just found out that the running total mileage for 'The Challenge' is 6219 with over £35,000 raised with more to come I expect, amazing.

The Neuro Surgical team, minus Neil, step into the room. We have a brief chat about me and how I am feeling and then it is time for the big reveal, I sit in the chair and one of the team positions himself behind me, the others line up in front of me just like the bridesmaids at a wedding waiting to catch the bouquet although I think it may be my head, they are there to catch. Gently he starts to remove the bandage, I hadn't realised just how tightly it was wound, the sensation of freedom I'm experiencing is wonderful.

He finishes and then examines the wound which he declares to be.

'Healing nicely.'

He continues.

'You can go home today; I will do the paperwork now and then you'll just be waiting for pharmacy to sort out your medication.'

 I thank them all for their help and concerns and then ring Anna to come and collect

A Matter Of Concern

I have only been home a few days and I receive a letter from Alan. He is writing to inform the group that since the trial finished, two of the participants have had significant problems, relating to the drug delivery system.

Now that there has been a third very recent problem, and he felt that it was important to update us on the possible risks or benefits of keeping the system in place.

In all three cases there had been infections around the port site during the trial. In two cases the ports had been removed leaving the internal tubing in place, and in the third case the system was still in place three developed infections which then tracked down to the catheter tip in the putamen.

At the beginning of the trial, it had been planned to remove the drug delivery system at the end of the trial if GDNF infusions did not continue. However, during the course of the trial the thinking on this changed given that the vast majority of the systems had been well tolerated and the port skin interface had been very stable, it was decided that rather than subject the participants to another general anaesthetic and brain surgery, the systems could safely be left in place.

So, at the end of the trial we were given the choice of either having our systems removed or to leave them in place. As at the time there was a remote possibility of future GDNF infusions I had opted to leave my system in place.

Alan continues to say that over the course of the next few weeks all of the participants will be reviewed on an individual basis and offered advice on their personal situation. He clarifies that it is thought that having your system removed will not impair having a further system implanted in the future.

He finishes on a personal note to say that as I have very recently had my entire system removed then no further action is needed in my case.

I read the letter again, our first concern should be the health and welfare of the participants. If there is a problem with the delivery system then measures need to be in place to prevent any more incidences occurring.

There is of course another potential problem that may arise, in order for the proposed new trial to take place substantial investment will be required. If it is proven or maybe only suspected that there is a problem with the longevity of the delivery system, despite the fact that GDNF works any possible investors will disappear back into the woodwork.

The Celebration

It is now ten days since my surgery and I am recovering well, the wound is healing nicely and I am catching up on my rest.

There is only just over a week until the Challenge Celebration. I contact Jayne as I know that there are things that need to be done to ensure everything runs smoothly, she gratefully accepts my offer of help and I make a start collating the guests menu choices.

We are expecting around 130 guests and I have menu choices for nearly half of them, I have repeatedly asked for this information and yet here I am still emailing, texting or phoning guests. I am amazed at how many people reply claiming not to have received any menu information and then they proceed to give me their choices without asking to see a menu, I make a note that the lack of GDNF may be giving the participants telepathic powers.

It's three days later, between us Jayne and I have somehow managed to get everyone's choices. We have spent the last couple of days trying to contact all the guests, the task was further complicated by people changing their minds, are they staying over or not? Can they have a refund because some of their party can no longer make it? Can they have extra tickets?

All of this, of course, has an effect on the hotel charges and we have revised the figures many, many times eventually arriving at a sum that matches the invoice. Hurray. Only one more sleep until the event itself, despite all the work everyone is buzzing with anticipation. This will be the first time in over a year that we have all got together and for many of the Working Party the first time they will have ever met, apart from via our regular Zoom meetings. We have all become firm friends and the meetings often pass by in a whirl of banter and humour. Although glad that the ceaseless work has now come to an end, I shall certainly miss these meetings.

There is to be a meet and greet session between 2.00 and 4.00 p.m. in the hotel bar. Anna and I arrive early to help set the room up and organise the last-minute details. Slowly the room fills with a host of recognisable faces and although having only been together virtually before, the conversation flows and the time whizzes by. Unfortunately,

Jeff and Mary have not been able to attend, as they have tested positive for Covid 19, it's such a shame particularly as 'The Somerset Shakers and Shufflers', Jeff's team, have been one of the most productive teams covering over 600 miles. A zoom meeting has been set up with them so they are able to join with us virtually at least. I look at the clock and I'm surprised to find that it's 5.00 p.m. and we are due to meet back down in the bar at 6.00 p.m. So, we retire to our room, emerging just a few minutes later in all our finery. Making our way back through the hotel we reminisce about our youth, when we dreamt of running away to the Circus and becoming world-famous Quick-Change artists, we even had a stage name ready, 'Rollin's Rapid Robe Revolution'. Unfortunately, due to a particularly nasty accident with a mince pie during a Christmas performance our quick-change career was short lived. Luckily there was a doctor in the audience who gave me some cream for it, although I still bear the scars and a slight limp to remind us of what might have been.

As we arrive the first few guests are starting to appear in the bar, a few minutes later and the room is crowded. I scan the room and see our daughter, Sophie, easing her way through the throng towards us followed by the other members of our family. Jayne asks if we could start moving into the ballroom as we need to get the guests seated, we move off and as the people nearby notice they follow and within 15 minutes most of the guests are seated.

I look around, it's a large room with a capacity of 200, however 130 guests seem to fill it nicely leaving plenty of room for the 'Parkies' attending to stagger around unaided.

The guests are mostly people with some connection to Parkinson's, twentyish of the trial participants are in the room, Alan and Lucy along with some Nurses from the Bristol Brain Centre, representatives from Parkinson's UK, Funding Neuro and Cure Parkinson's, together with team members from the Challenge and so on. The room is filled with happy chatting and a warming party atmosphere.

The room becomes silent as the Mistress of Ceremonies, our very own Vicki opens the proceedings. The meal is served and in between courses we are treated to speeches by Lesley, the Charities, Jayne and Tom. Sue has

171

written a book of ditties and rhymes from which she reads out a slightly rude one which has the room in stitches. Next the comedian Paul Mayhew Archer shares with us half an hour of stories relating to the funny side of living with Parkinson's, yes there is one.

By now it's nearly 10.00 p.m. and local singer Ken Trowbridge takes to the stage and blasts out a set of popular songs from the 60's and 70's, the dance floor is full to overflowing all night, with the volume in the room increasing as people start to singalong. It's after midnight and Ken is showing us the way to Amarillo as a conga starts to snake its way around the room led by the Mistress of Ceremonies, normally the people following her stumble and shuffle along but now they are helping

172

each other to remain upright and doing their upmost to keep going until the music stops. Parkinson's is a terrible thing to live with, so given the opportunity or maybe it's down to the cocktail of drugs that most of us have rushing through our bodies, but these 'Parkies' certainly know how to have a good time.

The evening draws to a close, Ken has already done two encores, the remaining guests although totally exhausted would happily carry on all night, but alas the party's over.

Anna and I are down for breakfast early, we join Bob at a table and talk about the huge success the previous evening had been. Slowly we watch as the other guests emerge, most are walking a little slower than yesterday, but no one is complaining

This morning there is to be a meeting for the trial participants, to update us on all things GDNF related. At 10.00 a.m. we gather in a function room eager to make a start, Jayne and Lesley busy themselves setting up the Zoom link by which those who are unable to attend can join us.

Alan is the first speaker and he is running through the trial results to show us just how close we came to a successful outcome.

I will attempt to explain in plain English as it is an extremely technical subject.

Large pharmaceutical companies like treatments to have shown benefit to patients and to have met four criteria, without these criteria a treatment which was beneficial to some patients is not likely to be developed further due to the massive costs involved.

He continues. The first of these criteria is 'Did the drug reach the site in the brain where it was needed to have an effect?' in the case of GDNF, which is a growth factor, and needs to be applied to dopamine nerve cells to help them regenerate. This means that there must be a surgical approach to overcome the blood brain barrier. There is some good evidence that was achieved in the trial. With the MRI scans showing the spread of the GDNF over the necessary brain structures. So, we have delivery of the drug across the structure of the brain. That is the first criteria met.

The second criteria is 'Target tissue engagement' or ensuring that the drug locks onto the required receptor in the brain to cause nerve cell sprouting of damaged nerve neurons. This is where the infamous PET scans come into

175

place, these showed a biological response and that the drug has engaged with its receptor. It could also be seen that the later scans of patients with mid or later stage Parkinson's resembled scans of early-stage Parkinson's patients, which shows restoration of dopamine brain cells. Second criteria met.

The Third criteria is Functional Pharmacology, to achieve this you would have to be able to get the drug on the receptor which causes biochemical change. Some of the participants had restored dopamine release. Third criteria met.

And the fourth criteria is Relevant Phenotype or an improvement in outcomes. This is where despite how much improved the participants feel you need to be able to show an improvement using a recognised rating scale and unfortunately it was not possible to prove this in the trial. Better rating scales are currently being developed which will capture the data that the existing rating scales are missing.

So, 3 out of 4 criteria met, it is a bit like having the Beatles without Ringo, not complete but still able to play a tune.

It is annoying to have got so close and to be failed by a rating scale which is maybe outdated and in need of replacement.

We move on to viewing video footage of one of the participants 'off' medication assessments and the difference in his walking as the trial progress's is amazing, how anyone can watch this and then say that GDNF doesn't work is unbelievable. Alan has spoken for around an hour and a half to a captivated audience, this is the first time that the results have been explained in plain English. To have come so close to a successful outcome and fail is heart breaking, we must ensure that GDNF gets another chance to prove itself.

The next speaker is Sharon who works with Steven Gill, she updates us on his work only in very brief detail as his new approach is at the moment confidential, all I can say is that it looks promising.

We break for coffee and the next to speak are Emma and Cheney from the LEARN study, they are based in Cardiff and have travelled over today to update us on the study's progress. We have exchanged many emails and spoken via Zoom meetings last year when we were helping to develop the protocol for their study. This is the first time that we have actually met and I took the opportunity before the meeting started to have a chat, and remind them that I haven't been seen yet.

Emma and Cheney update the room. A large section of the participants have now been interviewed and large volumes of information imparted. At long last nearly five years after the trial had finished the participants have given up all the valuable data that they had been forbidden to talk about, even though the trial team were not allowed to collect it.

The last speaker is Claire from Parkinson's UK, she speaks for a few minutes on the progress of the new trial. Unfortunately, she is telling us old

179

news and there appears to be no urgency to get things moving.

The meeting ends and we say our fond farewells to each other, it's been a wonderful weekend which makes all the work over the last year or so worthwhile and the group is stronger as a result. It's not quite over for some of us Jayne, Darren, Lesley, Colin, Bob, Anna and I are staying over for one more night to give us a chance to go over things and slap each other on the back.

We are planning on going out for a meal later on and arrange to meet in the bar beforehand. As we sit enjoying a drink and the company Jayne gives us some breaking news that she only heard today. There has been a large donation made to the Bristol Brain Centre as a direct result of the

Challenge, the donor could not make the payment to the Challenge as it wasn't a charity and so the Brain Centre benefitted to the tune of £100,000, added to the Challenge total itself which has now risen to around £70,000.

What a finish to the Challenge!

New Year, New Hope Or No Hope?

Today is the 5th January 2022, the world at large has just celebrated the beginning of a new year. Most people are hoping that this year will be the start of the end of the Covid 19 pandemic, personally I don't think things will ever return to what was previously considered to be normal. The vaccine has made it probable that the NHS will not be overwhelmed and that's as good as it's going to get for the time being.

Today is also the fifth anniversary of me receiving my last GDNF infusion, which also marked the end of the trial for me.

Five years since the last trial finished and just about a year from Parkinson's

UK's announcement of their intention to commence stage 2 of their plan for GDNF and the current position regarding a new trial is, once again, stalemate. The company that was to provide the GDNF are distancing themselves from the project because they fear that if the new trial failed as well then, they could be hurt by any negative publicity. Also, Renishaw who own the rights to the delivery system will not agree terms for its use in the trial. So, progress has once again ground to a halt.

Parkinson's UK it would appear are reverting to form and there is no sense of urgency at all, they are quite prepared to let the timeline slip. I believe that the basic difference between us is the fact that all the members of the participant's group

183

have to live with Parkinson's and are reminded every hour of every day of the desperate need for a cure. Whereas the Parkinson's UK team are employees who mostly work 9.00 to 5.00, 5 days a week. When they go home, all things Parkinson's stay in the office, for them there is always another day.

On a personal level I am about to retire, I'm 59 and have worked continually since I left school in 1979, nearly 43 years ago. Upon hearing the news that I'm retiring aged 59 most people say. 'How lovely, you're so lucky.'

I don't know how lucky it is to have a degenerative disease for which there is no cure, but never mind, it's the thought that counts. Anna and I decided at the beginning of 2021 that the time had come to make time for us and to do everything we want to while I still can. During my last appointment with Alan in November, I mentioned that I was planning to retire soon. Alan who had just examined me asked if I could retire immediately, as he was so concerned about my safety. He also told me that the time had arrived to consider different treatments and so I have recently been assessed for 'Deep Brain Stimulation'. This involves implanting electrodes within certain areas of the brain. These electrodes produce electrical impulses that regulate abnormal impulses within the brain.

The amount of stimulation is controlled by a pacemaker-like device, placed under the skin in your upper chest. A wire which travels under the skin connects this device to the electrodes in your brain. This is an advanced treatment for Parkinson's and is used when the traditional medications are no longer able to control the symptoms.

So, more brain surgery. This really is becoming a habit.

As part of this screening, I have to keep four day's worth of Parkinson's Disease diaries. This is a record of medication taken and whether you are asleep, on, off, on with dyskinesia and so on taken at half hour intervals. As I hand the diaries over to Lucy, I casually ask her. 'Why isn't there a column to record being off with dyskinesia.'

She stops what she is doing and replies.

'that's because you can't be off and have dyskinesia'

'However, It's something that some of the participants have developed'.

She continues and is promptly interrupted by another nurse with some concern about another patient, by the time she returns to the conversation it has moved on and I am about to undertake another 'off' medication assessment, I have completed these assessments many times before. The first one being as part of the preamble to the trial, on that occasion my UPDRS was 42 and on the latest occasion 40, if you factor in the assumed two points progression of disease per year allowance my score should be around 52 to 54.

So, I am still ahead of the game being as I am roughly the same score as I was nearly seven years ago. However, if this really is the case why am I considering having 'DBS'?

One of the failings of the 'UPDRS' system is that it is weighted towards certain symptoms such as tremor, which in my case is still greatly improved. Unfortunately, my other symptoms dyskinesia, freezing, posture, rigidity and walking have all worsened.

Overall, I am worse than before the trial but the UPDRS system cannot accurately measure this. Conversely it cannot accurately measure improvements either. The need for a better scoring system before the next trial begins is paramount.

4th February 2022

Anna & I are having a Zoom meeting this afternoon with Cheney from the LEARN study. She contacted me last week and we made arrangements. I must be one of the last participants to be interviewed, it's my fault, as I have been holding out for a face-to-face interview rather than a Zoom meeting. as I feel that I would be more forthcoming actually in the same room as the interviewer rather than over the internet.

With no ending in sight for the Covid restrictions, coupled with the strict outlook that the University of Cardiff has adopted throughout the pandemic means that there is no realistic alternative to a Zoom meeting.

At the allotted time I follow the link, Mr Zoom works his magic and Cheney appears in front of me, we greet each other and I introduce Anna.

To begin with she takes me back to when I was diagnosed, June 2010, 12 years ago, I was 47 and had gone to my GP's for the first time in years. I had a tremor but I was told.

'Not to worry, it's definitely not Parkinson's.'

This exchange marked the end of my confidence in GP's and I'm sorry to say nothing has happened since to change my mind.

We move on to my application to the trial, each question she asks leads to another and then she asks for more detail. Watching her work is amazing, you think you're having a chat but you are telling her your life story. She either did her training with Eamon Andrews or the Stasi, I'm not sure which, I will wait until we finish, she will either lock me up or give me a big red book.

We continue through the trial, afterwards and up to the present day. I look at the clock over three hours has passed in an instant, it's been an emotional time for both of us.

Revisiting some dark days and some happy ones, Anna tells Cheney of when I just announced that I was applying to go on the trial without any discussion at all and of her experience on the day I had the delivery device installed. Eight hours of hell not knowing what was happening, wondering to herself why was I undergoing experimental brain surgery when I didn't need to. This is a good example of the improvements in the participants care that we hope will emerge from this study, I should never have been allowed to sign up without more consultation with my family, after all they would have had to live with the consequences good and bad. I can blame only myself for this, as I was so

keen to be accepted onto the trial, I
would have virtually done anything.

The Concert & An Activation

It is now 10th May 2022. Anna and I are travelling north on the M5, our destination, Solihull. I am 4 weeks post-surgery after having had my DBS system installed. I cannot drive for another 2 weeks. However, due to the worsening of my condition I no longer enjoy driving. So, this is another burden that Anna has taken on.

A few weeks ago, Lesley got in touch to say that Paul Mayhew Archer is generously performing on behalf of the GDNF fund at Solihull School on 10th May. The evening is being arranged by the Solihull branch of Parkinson's UK, Jan, one of the organisers, who knows Lesley contacted her to see if any members of the group wanted to attend.

There was a surge of WhatsApp messages and a delegation comprising Jayne, Darren, Lesley, Colin, Vicki, Bob, Anna and I was formed to represent the group at large. All of us are taking advantage of the opportunity to socialise and are staying overnight.

We arrive at the hotel mid-afternoon shortly followed by Jayne and Darren, so we retire to the bar for a catch up. Although we have had Zoom meetings this is the first time, we have seen each other since the Challenge Celebration last October. We sit and spend a friendly couple of hours, happy in each other's company.

Jayne updates us on progress with the new trial, most of the elements are nearly in place. Agreement has been reached with Renishaw for the supply of the delivery device, there are two companies in place to manufacture the GDNF and progress with the regulatory bodies is ongoing. It really feels like this time the trial may be going to happen. However, in light of the problems encountered with the delivery device by some of the participants a safety review is currently being completed. This is tremendously important as we have to ensure that every aspect of the trial is as safe as possible for the future participants. Unfortunately, after all these years of campaigning for a new trial the results of this review will make or break it. If the review finds that there is a problem then the required investment will simply disappear. If this happens it will be the final nail in GDNF's coffin and the end of all our work. I would be devasted, but if GDNF can't be delivered in a safe manner using the existing system, who knows what will happen.

The afternoon has slipped away and we return to our rooms to rest before the performance.

It's a little before 6.00p.m. and we are meeting in the hotel foyer, by now Lesley, Colin, Vicki and Bob have joined us. It's a 10-minute walk to the theatre. So, we set off and arrive an hour or so later having stopped for something to eat enroute. Paul Mayhew Archer is chatting to the guests as they find their seats. A lady separates from the crowd and greets Lesley, this is Jan who is organising the event, she shows us to our front row seats and the audience settle down. Adjacent to the stage is a grand piano and on it are the raffle prizes and two piles of my book, which I have supplied for them to sell for the fund. Jan gives the audience a brief introduction of the group and then Lesley and Vicki get to their feet, they have been asked to say a few words about GDNF and what's happened since the end of the trial, they are well received.

Then it's time for the main event, Paul Mayhew Archer himself. The next hour disappears in a blur of laughter as he tells us of his experiences of Parkinson's and his comedy career.

It's now the interval and a queue is forming by the piano to buy raffle tickets, as people pass the piles of my book they stop, pick up a copy, leaf through it and read bits. I expect them to return the books to the pile, but no, some people are holding on to the book and then paying for it. A few ladies ask me to sign their copies, by the end of the interval nearly 20 books have been sold, how wonderful.

There is another hour of merriment then it's back to the hotel for a nightcap before bed.

21st May 2022

Mother has been planning a plant sale in aid of the GDNF fund for months and now the day has arrived. For the past few days, the weather has been cloudy with some very wet patches, but today has dawned bright and sunny. We have already spent the whole of yesterday preparing things for today, it's just after 08.00 am. and we are back again moving plants and so on. By10.00 a.m. the last few plants are still being put out, but it's time for the sale to begin. Mother has organised several of her friends and our family members to help out. One is taking the entrance fees, others are serving teas, coffee and cakes and a couple selling the plants. I am seated in the hallway with a notice board filled with information about GDNF and the group, I also have some copies of my book to sell. People have to pass me to get their teas and coffees, so I have a captive audience and spend a very pleasant few hours talking to people about the group's activities, GDNF and Parkinson's in general. A surprisingly large number identify themselves as people living with Parkinson's either a partner or family member, so we swap stories. All too soon the crowd's part and it's all over.

Grand total raised £538.00 Well done Mum.

It's now 25th May and we are in the car again, this time it is a short journey to

the Brain Centre. It's activation day for
my DBS system. As we travel, I receive a
text message from Darren wishing me
well, closely followed by a series of
WhatsApp messages from the rest of
the Working Party. As I read them, I
consider how nice it is to have friends
who are going through or have been
through similar situations and who can
offer advise based on their own
experiences. We arrive and a few
minutes later Lucy calls us in, and I
slowly shuffle through. I am off
medication and am well aware of the
fact, every step is a huge effort and by
the time I have got to the treatment
room I am exhausted. This is how it has
been for the last couple of months,
with Mr Parkinson's gradually trapping
me within my own body. It's like being
in a cellar and the trapdoor is closed. I
'm hoping that the DBS will be my key

to the trap door through which I can escape.

Already in the room is Oona who works for Medtronic, the company who manufactured the DBS system. It is a newish type of system and it has 'brain sensing', this is the ability to be able to record your brain waves in order to observe how your Parkinson's has been behaving recently. The brain sensing mode was activated when the system was installed and so has been recording my brainwaves for the last six weeks, all of this data should simplify the tuning in process and give more accurate results.

Lucy examines me in order to gauge my off-medication state, I touch her finger and then my nose, carry out foot stamps and slowly manage to complete some finger taps, then it's a slow shuffle with my walking stick up and down the hospital corridor before collapsing back into the chair. They wirelessly connect the device to a tablet and start to view the stored information. It sounds very complicated it's all alpha, beta and gamma waves. They are using the data to select the optimum settings for the system. They start with my left side and then my right, while the adjustments are being made, I have to sit as still as possible, as I do so I can feel the rigidity slipping out of my legs I imagine it running out of me and forming pools under my feet. I am watching the tremor in my right hand, as Lucy makes the adjustments it slows and then stops all together.

I am then re-examined, this time my finger taps are large and strong, my foot stamps echo around the room and the rigidity in my arms and legs has greatly improved. Then it's time for a walk, as soon as I stand, I can feel how much my balance has improved and as Lucy passes me my walking stick, I confidently tell her that I don't need it. I stand at one end of the corridor and start off, my steps are positive and purposeful, I'm lifting my feet clear of the floor and the steps are large. I reach the end of the corridor, turn sharply, and start back, the whole walk has only taken a few seconds, but it marks a defining moment in my Parkinson's. And in the absence of even the remote possibility of any GDNF in the near future, the DBS offers me the opportunity to have a breathing space in the slow decline of my condition.

I am over the moon, I haven't felt this good for years, probably since the GDNF infusions finished, five years ago.

The Statement

It is now September and the long hot summer days are gone. We have finally got what we want, at least weather wise, it's raining and has been for a few days. At least the gardeners are happy.

It is also just about a year since Alan wrote to us to explain about the incidents involving the delivery system and several months since the safety review was commissioned, we are still awaiting the results good or bad.

I receive an email from Jayne, she is calling a GDNF Working Party meeting for next week,

15th September, to discuss the results. In the mean-while, The Working Party

205

have recently been contacted by Emma
from the LEARN Study in Cardiff. They
have been working through the data
from all the interviews with the group,
in total over half of the participants
came forward to be interviewed by
them. They have found It to be
absolutely fascinating and are grateful
for all of the time given by the group.
They have asked the Working Party for
some help in producing some evidence-
based guidance for use in future clinical
trials, in particular a checklist for would
be participants consideration and
guidance for 'off' assessments and
scans. Both of which will ensure that
future participants will be better
informed than we were and more able
to make an informed decision. I glance
through the first draft for these
documents, they are impressive and
contain more questions that can be

asked about any future trial than I could ever have thought of. The 'off' medication guide is a revelation, although I knew what an 'off' period felt like I had no idea what it was called and would never have thought of asking for additional help to cope. There is talk of making part of the trial selection process an 'off' experience where possible participants can go 'off' before committing themselves. A check list or guidance is such a simple idea.

15th September 2022, Jayne has called a Working Party Zoom meeting and it's today at 10.00am, this is the first meeting for many months.

We begin with the usual catch up and then Jayne gives us an update on progress with the GDNF Involvement Advisory Board. This board was formed two years ago now and was set up specifically to ensure the views of people living with Parkinson's would be taken into consideration at the very heart of any potential GDNF trial design in the future. Jayne and Lesley are both members ensuring that the group's voice is heard and continues to be heard despite the rest of the board not necessarily wanting to hear it.

Apparently, the safety review on the delivery device has come back inconclusive and so the Board of Trustees of Parkinson's UK are going to be holding a meeting on 8th October, to decide if they will be moving forward with their plans for a new GDNF trial. Parkinson's UK have reluctantly agreed to allow the GDNF Participants Group to send a statement expressing our views for consideration by the Board.

The statement is prepared and it is decided that it would add gravitas if it is signed by as many participants as possible. So, I send out an email containing the statement asking if the group members are happy to add their signature to it. The response is incredible and I receive the first reply within minutes from Julia. Followed by a steady trickle over the next couple of days until we have twenty five positive replies, with only one participant declining to sign. That is amazing, we have had replies from people who despite having had many, many emails sent to them during the challenge they never replied to one. And yet here they are putting their support behind the statement, it really is heart-warming to get such a positive response, to know that despite everything that has happened and five plus years since the trial ended the participants still believe in GDNF. Unfortunately, amongst all the good news comes some bad, another member of our elite group, Ron who only wanted to be able to play football with his grandchildren, has passed away. This along with other members struggling with the toll that Parkinson's takes on our lives makes me realise for some our fight has already taken to long.

The Board of Trustee's decision is due on 8th October. Anna and I are going to be away, cruising which is unfortunate timing. Cruising has emerged as our ideal sort of holiday, you get the sunshine and travel whilst staying in a first class hotel, with plenty of dancing as well. As I say the ideal sort of holiday for us.

Since Covid 19 struck we have had three cruises cancelled. The first due to the pandemic, the next by us in September when I was having my GDNF delivery system removed and the last in May after my DBS surgery. This will be our first proper holiday for two years and we are looking forward to it, unfortunately communications are not great at sea unless you can afford one of the offered internet packages which at roughly £20.00 per day is a luxury we refuse to pay for. Besides the lack of communications is one of the elements of the holiday we like the most. However, our solitude may cause a problem this time. The only hope I have is to try and tag onto a local network when in port to hear the news.

Two days later and the ship is pulling alongside at the first port, my unusually silent phone starts to wake up, in the process spilling messages everywhere. I have missed the announcement and so download the link that Jayne has kindly provided, the message we have been anticipating appears before me and I quickly read it through before returning to reread it, this time more slowly to ensure that the contents are fully absorbed.

The Decision

Email to Group from Parkinson's UK;

PRIVATE AND CONFIDENTIAL

UNDER EMBARGO UNTIL 11 OCTOBER 2022, TIME TBC

HEADLINE: Making progress towards a potential new   GDNF trial

STANDFIRST: Over the last 2 years, Vivifi Biotech   has made progress towards a trial that aims to overcome the challenges of the last trial. Now, it's starting work on the final phase of planning.

STORY:

GDNF stands for glial cell-derived neurotrophic factor. It's a naturally-

213

occurring protein that is produced inside the brain. It supports the survival of many types of brain cells, including the cells lost in Parkinson's. We were the major funder of a pioneering trial that tested whether boosting levels of this restorative protein could slow, stop or reverse the progression of Parkinson's. In February 2019, we got the results. They were inconclusive, but there were some signs that the treatment may have started to regenerate participants' dopamine-producing brain cells.

In 2021 we announced that we would be investing up to £800,000 into Vivifi Biotech, a new company set up specifically to bring the focus and expertise needed to see if it was possible to plan and progress towards a new GDNF trial.

Today, we are announcing that Vivifi will be moving to the last phase of their work: seeking out partners to move GDNF towards another clinical trial.

A better understanding of the challenges

We have reviewed the scientific evidence from the first trial and listened to the views of people with Parkinson's about whether it is right to move ahead. There is still work that needs to be done on the device and drug manufacture to make sure they are the best that they can be. But the main focus for this can help make a future trial happen.

Arthur Roach, Director of Research, said:

"Through Vivifi Biotech's work in the last 2 years, we now have a better

picture of how GDNF might be studied further through a new clinical trial, and a specific plan that incorporates learnings from participants in the last trial, people with Parkinson's who might be asked to consider participating a new trial, and scientific and regulatory experts.

That includes a more detailed understanding of issues with drug supply and the device. And, we still believe that a new GDNF trial is possible.

"That's why we're continuing to invest in Vivifi to ensure that their work can keep making progress. We'll be monitoring their findings every step of the way, so like with every project in the Parkinson's Virtual Biotech, we can accelerate, pause or stop work as needed. And we'll be looking for

potential investors in the next stage of GDNF, alongside our other Virtual Biotech projects as part of a wider push for more investment in Parkinson's research."

The evidence is showing that there could still be a way forward for GDNF and finding investors needs to be the next priority. And that's why we're not stopping.

Informed by the community and experts

With what we now know, we believe that it could take around another 3 years to get to a trial, but we're continuing the work to make sure that the potential of GDNF is explored to its fullest.

We've always known that we wouldn't be able to take forward a new trial of GDNF alone.

217

Now with a better understanding of the estimated costs, we know we're looking for investors who can commit tens of millions of pounds.

Working towards new partners to help make it happen

Gary Shaughnessy, Chair of the Board of Trustees, said:

"In the last two years, with the insight and support of the GDNF Involvement Advisory Board that includes members of the Participants Group, consultation with people living with Parkinson's as well as scientific advisors, we have made real progress. Together we believe that GDNF has real promise, but there is still a long way to go before we can test it again in a clinical trial.

Finding investors to fund the very significant costs of a new trial is an immediate priority. We will be able to fund some of the

development ourselves but at this stage we need a partner who is willing to fund alongside us and to bring their expertise to help deliver a substantial and effective trial that is as safe as possible for all participants."

In the meantime, through the Parkinson's Virtual Biotech, we'll continue to invest in other projects too. Ones that can accelerate us towards other treatments, pursuing the most promising options available to us.

SIGNPOSTING / ONWARD JOURNEY:

The GDNF Participant Group

Formed when the trial ended, the GDNF Participant Group is a dedicated team of volunteers. Their campaigning and advocacy work champions further investigation into GDNF through raising awareness and funds for research.

So, it's a yes!!!!!!!!

I am slightly disappointed that the work of the Group is referred to only vaguely and in the last paragraph. After all the work, particularly by Jayne and Lesley, over the last few years to keep the hope of GDNF alive. When to everyone else it was an embarrassment which they would like to have been swept under the carpet.

The thought of another three years before the trial can start is daunting, that will be eight years since the last trial finished. What a waste of time, I wonder how many people with Parkinson's could have had an improved quality of life over that time if only the scientific world had listened, sooner. All the while the estimated cost has been steadily growing and now, they are looking for 'investors who can commit tens of millions of pounds'. There cannot be many people with that much spare change who want to invest in an unproven product, this I suspect, will prove to be problematic.

Overall, this really is excellent news, all the work over recent months is starting to pay off. The delivery of the message could have been a bit more passionate but, it is typical Parkinson's UK just the facts without emotion. Anna and I will certainly be celebrating tonight, splashing out on a couple of 'pussyfoots'. I assume that the rest of the Working Party will be doing similar. They certainly deserve it.

There are to be two- zoom meetings tomorrow, the first with the GDNF Participants Group to absorb the information and the second with Parkinson's UK to answer any questions. Fortunately, we are in port again tomorrow, I shall do what I can to join the first meeting for a few minutes before dinner.

The ship arrives in port the following morning and I am up early, downloading 'Zoom' onto my phone, I just hope it works. The meeting is set for 17.00 UK time, we are an hour ahead and the ship is due to sail at 18.00 so it's going to be tight.

I login to the meeting just before 18.00 and the ship is already moving away from the quay, I only have time for a quick 'Hello' and then the signal begins to break up, the picture goes fuzzy then disappears, I can text for a few more minutes and then that's it back to cruising with no signal.

Three days later I test positive for Covid 19 and am immediately confined to the cabin until the end of the cruise. I sleep solidly for the first day. Then slowly I begin to improve, and by disembarkation day I have gone stir crazy, maybe given another couple of days I would have joined a club with a social aspect to it, like say the slopping out club, and indeed look forward to the group activities.

The Fallout

Upon my return home I check my messages expecting to find congratulations and good will, but instead of the usual happy, chatty messages between the group. There is a definite chill. I contact Jayne to see why we are not celebrating.

Apparently, during the meeting Parkinson's UK closed the door on the early access to medicines for the participants, and some of them are bitter and cross about it. Also, it was felt that Parkinson's UK gave a very lacklustre performance, were vague in their answers and not at all interested.

Personally, I have given up on the early access to medicines a long time ago. Yes, it would be very nice to have a second bite of the GDNF cherry. However, I do what I do, 'in case', by this I mean 'in case' my children or other family members and friends are one day taken into a doctor's surgery and told that they also have Parkinson's.

The reports of Parkinson's UK's attitude tallies with feedback from the GDNF Involvement Advisory Group, which seems to have no structure capable of delivering a trial, decisions are left unmade and progress is slow. It has also been discovered that 'The LEARN study have not been invited to have any input into the new trial. This is surprising considering that it was funded by Parkinson's UK and that it's primary role is to provide assistance to groups setting up trials and studies to ensure that the participants have the benefit of those who have gone before, this is indeed strange behaviour.

The problems within the GDNF Participants Group must be dealt with first. Some of the participants now believe that the delivery system is too problematic to proceed with. A few are now promoting various other trials and research as the way forward, unfortunately none of which is closer to fruition than GDNF, with most being several years behind it. One participant, in his anger has sent an email to Gary, Chair of the board of the Trustees for Parkinson's UK, within which he accused the Board of all sorts of misdeeds, none of which were very complimentary. This has damaged our already fragile relationship and on a personal level upset and hurt people who are genuinely doing more than required to keep this GDNF monster moving towards a new trial.

Jayne and Lesley, who are the most involved with Parkinson's UK and have been responsible for all that has gone into building, what had been, a good working friendship. five years in the making, it has in an instant been damaged, a lot of trust has been lost and we are going to have to work hard to regain it.

There is concern amongst the Working Party that we are no longer representing the group's thinking, if true and we are far away from the group's consensus then we will no longer be able to represent them.

A meeting is called for the Working Party and it is decided to go to the polls to see if we still have the confidence of the wider group to deliver what they want. Over the next couple of days, a statement is produced which we plan to send to the group. We state what we believe to be the group's aims. To ensure that GDNF gets another chance to be proven in a clinical trial, this is our primary aim. In order to achieve this, we will support whatever delivery system is deemed to be the most suitable, currently we believe that it is still the convection delivery device used in our trial. As a secondary aim we will pursue the 'Early Access to Medicines Scheme' for the participants, but this would still only be a secondary aim.

We must ensure that the rest of the group understand and support this or it will not be fair to represent Personally, I am convinced that GDNF and the delivery system are still probably the treatment which is the nearest to clinical use currently available for Parkinson's. We know that GDNF works and the delivery system is tried and tested, therefore we have a workable treatment. The delivery system may not be perfect but it works and so let us use it to get GDNF proven.

The statement is sent with instructions to send back an answer yes or no would they like us to continue to represent the group based on the 'aims' statement.

We don't have to wait long before the replies start to arrive in my inbox, some simply say 'Yes' as requested others have added extra words thanking the Working Party for all their efforts and hard work. It's nice to be appreciated.

There is only one dissenter and they are advocating a different delivery system. So, not 100% but close.

We now need to wake Parkinson's UK from their slumber. A couple of choicely worded emails are sent to key players at Parkinson's UK, yet again outlining our concerns about the lack of direction, leadership, and discernible progress. They seem to be just going through the motions with no obvious plan to progress the trial onwards.

We hear back within a few days and are told that the GDNF Involvement Advisory Group, will be having a shake up with new members with experience of living with Parkinson's, they would like some to be participants and others who may want to be participants with the new trial. Roles within this group are to be clearly defined and support given where necessary.

It's a start, there is still so much that needs to be done to try and get this new trial up and running. I feel a bit overwhelmed, after all we are only a group of volunteers doing what we can to try and improve things for future participants, and so ask a question, although I already know the answer.

'Who did all of this work for our trial?' the reply comes back.

'No one, the work simply was not done.'

And I suspect that if it could have been forgotten about, it wouldn't have been done this time either.

It is very nearly Christmas and the group are making plans for a meet up in the New Year, which I am looking forward to. However, I think back to last Christmas and where we were then. The only progress that has been made is the safety review of the delivery device which has been completed and we have a decision to proceed with the new trial. I just hope that next Christmas the trial is up and running, hopefully? Although in the cold light of day it seems that we maybe dreaming the impossible dream.

16th January 2023, another New Year has dawned in a world where GDNF is not able to help Parkinson's sufferers. It's so frustrating to know that a treatment that could be used is sitting on a shelf gathering dust while people struggle with everyday life.

Personally, the only remnant of GDNF that is still working for me is the improvement in my tremor. Which over the course of the trial went from being extremely bothersome and uncontrollable to hardly noticeable and has, thankfully stayed that way. This one symptom improvement was worth all of the heartache on it's own. Why can't other people have the same benefit?

Today, is the first meeting of the revamped GDNF Involvement Advisory Group is being held at the 'Shard' in London. It is a very prodigious location for the meeting and I don't know if it marks a more determined approach from Parkinson's UK or if it's just a 'jolly'.

A couple of weeks later and we hold another Zoom meeting where Jayne and Lesley update us on the 'Shard' meeting. Generally, they are pleased with some of the improvements. However, there are many more things which should be going on and yet are not. We have been given the task of populating a document detailing our wish list of 'pre', 'during' and 'post-trial' support requirements for new trial participants, these are the things which should have been in place for us but were not.

The feeling around the virtual room is that although this work is important the Working Party are being side lined and have been allocated the task to keep us mute. A discussion follows on our personal feelings regarding the possibility of a trial actually taking place, as usual we all have similar perspectives and it is not good news. The overall view is that we still cannot understand why Parkinson's UK appear to be dragging their feet, they have no clear plan for a way forward and the leadership is non-existent. A major problem to us is the lack of potential investors, we are going around in circles. At the beginning of our struggle we said that we would do everything we could to give GDNF another chance to be proven, the feeling today is that we are fast reaching that point and that if things have not progressed in a years time, then we will re-focus our campaigning in a different, as yet, unknown way.

The meeting breaks up and I immediately set to and produce a list of trial support requirements, as requested, we are in the middle of a game with Parkinson's UK and it's a game we cannot lose.

Pre-trial support

1.   Once selected for trial, would be participants and carers to have

mandatory sessions with previous participants and their carers to ensure that would be participants can ask any questions which clinical staff cannot answer. Care should be taken to ensure there is no possibility of the placebo effect, guidelines on suitable and unsuitable subjects for discussion to be supplied. This may be achieved with the use of videos or Zoom meetings.

2.   The provision of a named member of staff to act as participant liaison for each participant, they would meet during the selection process and from then on be responsible for all appointments and act as a point of reference for all things trial, a friendly face to speak to over the phone at key stress moments such as providing updates during the delivery system surgery. Someone to ensure taxis arrive

on time and the participant is always kept up to date.

3.   Participants to visit key hospital areas such as infusion rooms, PET and MRI scanners with staff on hand to answer any questions or concerns that they may have. To explain the scanning process, time periods etc.

During trial care & support

1.   Every 12 weeks all participants to undergo a full medical examination, including suitable scans, to pick up early signs of port site infections etc. anyone found to have infection to be temporarily excluded from trial until they are declared to be medically fit , free from infection.

2.   All participants to have regular, suggest every 12 weeks, counselling

sessions to ensure that they are coping with the rigors of the trial.

On-going post trial care & support

1.   All participants to have delivery system removed completely within 6 months of end of trial, there should be a 'remove by' date included in the consent documentation. Once removed there should be on-going care, including scans, for a minimum of 2 years at 12-week intervals.

2.   If at the scheduled end of the trial it is decided to extend the trial participants, if they agree to continue, should be given a new 'remove by' date and all on going care extended by the length of trial extension.

3.   All participants & carers / partners, within 4 weeks of end of trial,

should be de-briefed, to help ease them back into normal life again. This will provide an opportunity to pass on contact information for support network.

4.   A support network to be established, which all participants and their carers are encouraged to join, with a nominated person who will remain in post for say two years post trial. During this time part of the nominated persons role will be to help establish a 'participants & carers community'. This community should be encouraged to be self-running by the end of post-trial period and will become the basis of a support network for the participants and carers. Financial support should be made available to facilitate this.

5.   Participant's GPs to be given training on port care and a point of contact 24/7 for emergency port problems, with financial inducement if required.

On-going post infusion assessments& updates

1.   Once the infusion stage of the trial has finished, i.e. the participant has received their last infusion, there should be an extended assessment period to ensure that any improvements that the participants experience post trial are accurately recorded. These assessments could be linked to the 12 weekly health checks previously mentioned and should run for a minimum of 18 months post trial, possibly longer if it is found to be informative.

2.	Trial results to be communicated to participants promptly and in plain English.

3.	Updates on trial news to be given on a monthly basis

4.	Once blinded phase of trial completed participants should be encouraged to socialise and social events planned.

I end up with a long list, it would be nice to protect future participants with these conditions but I foresee a long battle to get them included, but we must push on.

World Parkinson Congress

It is now April, and after all the rush to get the 'trial support requirements' prepared and submitted they have been forgotten. Personally, I think that it was just another task to keep the Working Party quiet, whilst at the same time giving an illusion of progress being made. We are now a third of the way through yet another year and apparently no nearer a trial.

Our wonderful Vicki has had a brainwave, fed up with the endless waiting she has taken the bull by the horns and stepped outside the box, she wants to attend the 'World Parkinson Congress.' To meet and mingle with the influential Parkinson's community who will be attending and generally promote the GDNF cause.

This really is a truly wonderful idea from one of the most passionate members of the Working Party, she is fed up waiting for Parkinson's UK and wants to appeal directly to those people who count in the Parkinson's world, who knows who she will end up speaking to and maybe that person will have a contact for funding, anything is possible. It can certainly do no harm, and is probably one of a very few opportunities left for us to pursue.

After a few brief ' Whatsapp ' messages it is decided that Vicki will be accompanied by Jayne and Darren and joined by Andy H, the only non-participant member of the Working Party who was invited to join after proving himself invaluable during the Challenge. He is attending the Congress already as a volunteer and will help during his time off. Together they are the GDNFer's version of the 'Fantastic Four' all with super powers attuned to our cause.

A major stumbling block could be funding with each delegate costing around £500.00 plus travel and accommodation. Fortunately, when asked, both Parkinson's UK and Funding Neuro have agreed to cover the costs.

The World Parkinson Congress is a world-wide meeting place for people concerned with the health and welfare of people living with Parkinson's disease and their families and caregivers. This year it is being held in Barcelona between 4th – 7th July, although it is packed full of seminars and so on the main approach to get the GDNF message across will be what's known as 'networking' or what used to be called speaking to people, and developing those relationships.

The Showcase

It is the first few days of June and the Working Party have been invited by Emma and Cheney from the LEARN Study to attend a Zoom meeting which will launch their results. Firstly to a select few on 5th June and then to the world at large on 12th June, they also are attending the World Parkinson's Congress in Barcelona to showcase their new resources.

The meeting on the 5th is a subdued affair and attendance is low, the Cardiff team have produced a series of excellent leaflets and videos, which star Jayne, Darren, Lesley and Colin all based on information gleaned from the participants during all those interviews. They are professional in appearance and ask more questions than I could

246

ever have thought of asking and with more to follow they really will be a valuable resource for anyone considering taking part in a clinical trial.

In passing it is mentioned that Cure Parkinson's are hosting an event within the next few weeks concerning all things GDNF and the GDNF Participants Group have either been forgotten or simply left off the guest list. This is very frustrating, when so much has been put into the current situation and then to be treated without any respect is disappointing. Jayne fires off a polite but to the point email asking if a representative from the group can attend. The reply when it arrives fobs her off, I can't believe we   are disliked so much that there is no room at the table for us. It must be what we represent, perhaps no one wants to sit

247

next to us, like the slightly mad spinster aunt at a wedding who ends up sat by the toilets talking to herself. Maybe we need to work on our social skills.

Our plans for the World Parkinson's Congress are well under way, hotels and flights are booked. We have leaflets explaining the group's role in the GDNF story and the current state of play, business cards with contact details having been printed, all thanks to Funding Neuro. Our   delegates are going to be wearing GDNF branded t-shirts to finish off the image, so I collect a couple of spares from local group members and that's it they are ready to go with time to spare.

12th May 2023, today is the webinar to officially launch the LEARN Study results, there is to be another launch at the World Parkinson's Congress, but this is the one that counts. I log on at just before 3.00pm and I'm greeted by Emma and Cheney, they go through the running order for the next hour or so. They are kicking things off themselves by giving a background to the study, telling of all those Zoom meetings throughout the pandemic, the interviews and finish off by showing the videos that they have produced as the resource which will be available to anyone planning a trial. They cover such an array of subjects such as scans, PET, MRI what to expect, questions to ask, timings and so forth. Other subjects include consenting, pre and post care with more in the pipeline.

They thank the group and the Working party in particular and move on to Lesley who is the next speaker, she speaks from a participants view point and shares some of the highs and lows of her experiences, as she finishes Jayne readies herself to tell of her experiences as a carer, though the term now is support provider which is nicer and a more accurate description of what is given so readily by so many partners, friends or family to us lucky few.

And then, direct from his busy clinic it's Alan Whone. It's a few months since I last saw the charming doctor and he's his usual cheery self. He is speaking about trials from a chief investigators side of things, he talks of what perhaps could have been done differently or better if they had had access to a resource such as the LEARN study. He mentions after care, better communications, having a plan B for when things go wrong.

He tells us of one entrant who whilst being consented for over two hours said that she would probably agree to anything to have the chance of a cure and that that it was akin to being consented at gun point. He continues to tell of how the LEARN study emerged from the aftermath of our study to provide a better trial experience for participants. He moves on to talk of the PD sensors study which was held in the Sphere house and along with several other GDNFer's, Anna and I participated in it. This was all about providing better, more accurate assessment tools using electronic devices and has recently been awarded £7 million to continue it's work. Although deemed a failure he talks of the many successes the trial had;

The delivery device was proven to be safe and capable of delivering drugs with pin point accuracy and has now been used in the treatment of tumours and brain cancers.

Infusions of GDNF have been proven to be tolerable.

The interesting PET scan results.

He reflects on, given hindsight, how things could have been handled differently post-trial as part of his reflections he mentions how some participants have been having dyskinesia in the 'off' state, of how this should not be happening unless he suspects that the sprouting seen on the PET scans has developed into dopamine producing brain cells. Although fully awake I am fully immersed in what Alan is saying and it takes a few seconds to absorb it, this is exactly what happened to me and the same conclusion I came up with back in 2018, 5 years ago. At the time I approached Parkinson's UK about being assessed again because I felt so strongly that I was holding the key to something and didn't want to lose the information, only to be told 'to go away, you are of no scientific interest'. Turns out I was right after all.

If only provision had been made for post-trial assessment. The trial would still have failed to meet it's primary end point due to the use of the UPDRS assessment tool. But the fact that my newly grown brain cells were producing dopamine roughly two years after my last infusion would have been discovered and dealt with appropriately. I wonder if the fact that I have dyskinesia when I am 'off' is an indication that my brain cells are still producing dopamine, I guess we will never know for sure!

The rest of the webinar passes in a bit of a blur, I am happy in my thoughts and email Jayne to thank her and tell her how much I have enjoyed the meeting.

I sit and think back over the last five and a half years to January 2017 when for me the trial finished, of how the GDNFer's came together, of how our aims were forged and their current position;

Another chance for GDNF to prove itself. This is now nearer than its ever been or likely to be.

A better trial experience for participants. With the LEARN team's announcement this is delivered.

Better assessment tools which capture the relevant information. With Alan's announcement regarding future funding this is delivered.

I think to myself as Meatloaf used to say ' Two outta three ain't bad' and with the third, the trial, possibly nearer than ever before, I think that we shall leave our ponderings for now.

The End?

When people ask me.

'Is the new trial going to start?'

Usually, I say things are progressing or something similar, but the honest truth is I don't know if or when its likely to be. Yes, there is progress but at less than a snail's pace. You can now say 'GDNF' in polite company without getting dirty looks and people want to be associated with it, which is a big improvement. When the GDNFer's first came together, to say GDNF was like saying 'Macbeth' in a theatre, people would cross themselves, rub their rabbits foot, touch wood and so on. Because it was deemed to have failed the scientific world was scared of being tarred with the same brush when it should have been embracing the results, that way all the positives that have now emerged would have been discovered earlier, instead we have lost several years which cannot be reclaimed.

There is hope that a new trial will be starting 'soon'. However, if we have learnt anything from this saga its that some things cannot be hurried. The GDNF Working Party remain hopeful but it is becoming more and more difficult to be positive, but we shall continue with our task until either the last hope is extinguished or a trial is under way.

Although in my humble opinion GDNF is a miracle treatment of biblical proportions and the delivery system, which was proven in our trial, is at the moment, the best way forward and

257

should be used now to get GDNF itself approved. Once approved the means of getting GDNF into the correct location can be tweaked and who knows what future technologies may be able to produce. With the cost of a trial ever sky rocketing, currently around £26 million, we must be careful that time does not erode GDNF's cost effectiveness and make an expensive treatment unaffordable in an NHS which is already under strain. It shouldn't happen but many health care decisions are based on cost not need

Rest assured while we can the GDNFer's will continue, to push to make GDNF available to those who need it.

Personally, my Parkinson's continues it's downward spiral, every positive seems to have a consequence, the latest being my DBS. which has been absolutely brilliant with my mobility but has affected my speech, which I find extremely frustrating.

Jayne recently asked me.

'Would you still have GDNF again if given the opportunity?'

I thought for a moment of everything that has happened since that day in March 2015 when I 'expressed an interest'. The highs and lows, of the treatment which had effectively cured me being taken away, of the friends I made along the way, of the new experiences I've had and of my hope for the future. I smiled at her and replied.

'Yes, I would'

In the meantime, like 'Clint Eastwood' in all of those spaghetti westerns the

GDNFer's will be riding off into the sunset towards the World Parkinson's Congress in Barcelona and then onwards and upwards to the next opportunity to spread the GDNF gospel.

Thank you for reading the latest in my tale of woe, I hope that you have enjoyed it, maybe someday I will be able to finish it with a happy ending, who knows.

A Turn Of Events

Well, that was where I was planning on leaving this book but upon their return from the Congress our team of intrepid delegates brought with them news of a highly successful GDNF trial which had been held in America recently, they have overcome the blood brain barrier problem by using gene therapy.

They are using viruses to 'infect' brain cells with GDNF genes, which in turn will make GDNF producing brain cells. The need for invasive brain surgery and repeated infusions is removed, with the gene being delivered in a one-off procedure after which the wound is closed greatly reducing the chance of infection.

There has been a small-scale phase 1 trial, which was successful with the treatment being found to be safe and well tolerated up to 5 years afterwards.

The existing study is open label with no placebo group. However, a larger blinded study is currently being planned.

The delegates excitement spreads around the remaining members of the Working Party as we can all see this treatments potential after a successful trouble free period of 5 years.

It is decided to contact the team behind this trial and offer our help and support. Within a couple of days Jayne receives a very positive reply, thanking us for getting in touch and offering to set up an introduction meeting, they also mention that they are 'keenly aware of the amazing and tightly knit

GDNF Participant Group' and are keen to set up links between us. Wonderful news.

This leaves us in the unusual position of the possibility of there being two GDNF trials in the pipeline, with two vastly different delivery systems.

Firstly, the convection-enhanced delivery system as used in our trial. Which remains in place throughout the treatment, this is a proven system, it is safe and tolerable although some participants had problems with infections.

And secondly there is gene therapy, where the GDNF is administered as a virus in a one-off procedure, greatly reducing the risk of infection. However, there is no 'off switch,' once the gene is in place it cannot be removed.

Both systems have had successful stage 1 clinical trials and had/have the potential for even better results at stage 2. The convection-enhanced delivery system failed its stage 2 trial despite many participants reporting 'miraculous' results and a new trial for the gene therapy is currently being planned. Both systems need a successful stage 2 trial before they can proceed along the road to approval. Ultimately the delivery system is secondary, if GDNF can be delivered to people with Parkinson's in a safe way, once inside those brains the GDNF can work its magic. Which will in my opinion be as good as a cure. In the meantime the GDNF Participants Group will continue to offer support and it's talents where ever we are needed.

Unfortunately, and I hate to say it out loud but I think that it is still going to be 5 – 10 years before 'the wonder drug' will be available.

The Supremes said 'You Can't Hurry Love' it also appears that 'You Can't Hurry Science'.

Please prove me wrong.

Please visit The GDNF Participant's updated website for all things GDNF;

www.gdnf.org.uk

About The Author

Andy still lives near Bristol, since his last book he has gained a Grand Daughter and lost a job, as he is now retired. He lost his lifelong, 43 years, job in the fight against Parkinson's when it became too much of a struggle to continue. He fills his time babysitting, dancing, and attending hospital appointments. He is enjoying his new found freedom with his lovely wife. His belief in the magical properties of GDNF continues.

Printed in Great Britain
by Amazon

33081349R00157